A MAGICK REALITY?

AN
EXPERIMENTATION
AND EXPLORATION OF
THE LAW OF ATTRACTION

Copyright Year: 2008 Angelica Lyte

Copyright Notice: by Angelica Lyte.

All rights reserved. No part of this publication may be reproduced or transmitted in any form or by any means, electronic or mechanical, including photocopying, recording or by an information storage and retrieval system, without permission in writing from Angelica Lyte. Reviewers may quote brief passages.

The above information forms this copyright notice: 2008 by Angelica Lyte. All rights reserved.

ISBN Number: 978-0-9558541-0-1

Prefix number: 978-0-9558541

IN LOVING MEMORY OF SCOTT MICHAEL STACEY

AND

A DEDICATION TO MY FOUR BEAUTIFUL CHILDREN

INTRODUCTION

Quantum Physicists have been making some fascinating discoveries concerning atoms and our universe. Everything around you, including yourself, is made up of atoms. If you look at your hand under a microscope you can see we are made up of atoms. Scale down and look even closer and one can see the energy. Experiments held by top scientists have revealed that when no one is looking at the atoms they act like waves (they are waves of possibility). However, when someone is looking at them they respond by acting as the person watching them expects them to act. They take on the form that the person, viewing them with the visible eye, expects to see. The person observing therefore creates his or her own reality. We are in fact co-creators of this world and we shape our reality with our expectations; the thoughts we habitually hold. Thoughts do actually shape our future experiences because we attract whatever we focus on and whatever we are sending out into the universe. The universe is indeed like a mirror that reflects our inner feelings and thoughts.

The film '*What the Bleep do We (K)now!?*' reveals that thought waves have a frequency. Thoughts are creative energy and energy equals matter according to *Albert Einstein's* theory. Scientists have run tests that reveal positive thoughts are a thousand times more powerful than negative ones. They have also discovered that the

INTRODUCTION

mind cannot distinguish the difference between what you imagine in your mind and what is real. If you imagine what you want vividly, with love and lots of energy, it will manifest because the outside world always reflects the inside.

Scientists are now finding their theories parallel with the claims of religious, spiritual and ancient beliefs that all claimed the law of attraction is the law of the universe. You attract what you think or feel about most so if you think about negative things constantly then you can guarantee that you will get negative experiences occur constantly in your life. The trick is to re-programme yourself because so far all of your life you have been conditioned and programmed by the illusion, the negativity and the media to name but a few. You live on default by continually relating your present circumstances/experiences to the past. However, this will stop when you become aware of your full potential and the revelation hits you that you really do create your reality.

If you make a conscious effort to constantly think about things from a positive perspective or focus on what you do want, instead of what you do not want, one can begin to build a new neuron network in the brain. Every time you think a positive thought a positive seed is planted and grows until eventually all the negative

INTRODUCTION

thoughts are replaced by positive ones. Soon your mind will naturally choose the best possible outcome of every situation. It will choose positive thoughts and feelings by default.
The brain will rewire so-to-speak. It is important, when you start trying to consciously replace negative thoughts with positive ones, that the process is fun. Focusing on love and feeling love when trying to manifest your desires is crucial.

The law of attraction has also been described as '*The Secret*' because this information has been kept a secret from the people throughout history in order to control them and stop us from becoming empowered. Knowledge equals enlightenment after all. Although books have been written about the law of attraction, what they did not actually tell us is that what we actually think about is literally what we get!!! Or that our thoughts are very powerful and are responsible for everything we experience and bring into our lives!!! I recommend you watch the film '*The Secret*' if you want to understand more about how to apply the secret and manifest anything you want and desire. Like many other people across the world I am now keeping a diary in order to explore whether the law of attraction really exists and works. Like many other people I wish to manifest the man of my dreams and I hope to do this by consciously and carefully applying the law of attraction

INTRODUCTION

successfully. I also wish to become successful and wealthy. It is my intention that this book is successfully published and can help other people to manifest the man or woman of their dreams too.

During this exploration I will in a sense attempt to re-brainwash myself using positive affirmations, visualisation and meditation. I have also created a holographic focus point full of images to focus on (Visit my site www.piczo.com/AngelicaLyte to view this) which I use to envision my desires as if they are already happening. Making one of these vision boards helps speed up the creation process. In other words it helps to manifest your desires because you put energy into it. I have also enjoyed creating two magic love vision videos on U-Tube which I watch every day. It is also a good idea to write down a list of qualities you wish to find in your ideal soul mate. (See Appendix A) I have read that it is a good idea to carry this list around with you. But Why? Find out later in this diary. You will be amazed when you find out the reason is connected to water. It is also worth remembering that if you believe this notion then yes, it is a good idea to carry it around with you because belief is the key that unlocks the door. Although you may have previously read or heard that you should write down the qualities you wish to find in your soul mate, I doubt this information stressed the importance of being precise. A very

INTRODUCTION

important point I wish to make to you and heavily stress, is that you must not focus on anything negative. Time and time again people write lists detailing what they do not want in their ideal soul mate. For example do not write 'I do not want an alcoholic'. If you focus on this, whether you want it or not, then this is what you will get! Negatives cannot enter the picture of what you want for yourself whatsoever. So be very careful about what words you choose and what you think about. List positive attributes only and remember if you want him to be local then write this down. Also love yourself so that you become lovable. It is worth mentioning again that our expectations affect our reality. Our beliefs, our faith or lack of it, create our life and the world we perceive. So if you believe you will never meet your soul mate then you probably never will, but if you believe that you are already connected and that you are destined to be together then you will be. (Will being the operative word – WILLPOWER)

Another word of advice is to never dwell on the past unless its good and you want more of the same. Let go of the past or you will forever be recreating it. There are trustworthy, loving, wonderful people out there. There is marriage material out there. There is someone out there, sitting there, reading this thinking and wanting the same things as you. Visualise what you want, let go and forget

INTRODUCTION

you even asked. Know that your wish is already granted and be grateful for your new husband or wife. Thank the universe. Gratitude is really important and the more reasons you can find to be grateful for and acknowledge that gratitude, the faster and better the results in your life will become. Only ever think about your wish as if it has already happened from the moment you wish it until the moment it manifests. Also remember that practise makes perfect and confirm that whenever you are able to successfully manifest one fantasy/desire/thought then you are able to build bigger and better dreams into a reality.

MANIFESTATIONS

Before I seriously started to write this diary I made a note of the manifestations that appeared during the three months after I watched the film '*The Secret*' which revealed how to apply the law of attraction. There was so much evidence of the law of attraction and manifestations that I felt I needed to write a diary plus I wanted to share my findings. So before you take a look at my diary have a peek at these:-

Gifts – I have been given gifts left, right and centre (things I need and desire from perfume to flower pots.

Ten Pences – I started on small amounts as believable and I could not believe the amount of ten p's I kept finding everywhere.

Money Spiders – I wanted to magic money spiders and kept finding them on me.

My friends came over and focused on my spider webs and lo and behold they manifested more. My son is obsessed with spiders and continually manifests them in my home.

Pictures for my vision board – Came through post free

MANIFESTATIONS

Feathers – Visuals on U-Tube included images of feathers and lo and behold feathers began to manifest everywhere I looked.

My Garden – Everything in it came through form. Transformed from mud to paradise

Parking – I visualise parking spaces empty before I go out and it works.

Mattress – Got mattress after seeing an ad in the shop window. This took a few weeks to manifest.

Trousers – Sent out this wish for a particular pair of trousers about a year ago when I gave away a pair that I really liked. It was not until I knew the LOA that these manifested.

Electric – Went to the shop to get electric, but I knew I did not have enough to pay back the emergency (which I had to do before it would give me any electric) so I asked the universe for a miracle. As I stepped into the shop I watched the miracles unfold in front of me. The two shop assistants were rushed off their feet. I was being served when a man came in and asked the shopkeeper, who was serving me, to help him do his daughter's hair (he was holding the

MANIFESTATIONS

fort as his wife had just had a baby) The shopkeeper accidentally keyed in that I wanted £20 electric and she tried to undo this mistake. However, she could not and I suggested that I could pay for it another time seeing as she was so busy. Of course this was to her satisfaction considering she did not know whether she was coming or going and it was certainly to my satisfaction. I was extremely in awe of the miracle that took place and very grateful.

Money - £150 out of the blue child tax credit that was underpaid was given to me

Two Holidays – I won these from two scratch cards.

Good Sequences of Events have occurred – Things falling into place nicely.

Men – Back in March I went to a party and I met a particular person there who i liked.
At this particular time I had been sending out the wish for a dark attractive man. However, after the party I let go of thinking about this man. In September, five months later, after creating my wish with the thoughts I held, this man was trying to get my phone

MANIFESTATIONS

number after I again bumped into him. It took five months for my wish to materialise, without putting any effort into it, merely using thoughts.

Also a man I met in August on the internet, who was dark, asked to meet me. His name was Paul and I had to chuckle because in my novel '*Please Believe!*' the protagonist, Precious, meets a man called Paul before she meets the man of her dreams so I did not want a Paul. When I wrote '*Please Believe!*' (the sequel to '*Precious*'), the last part of the book was used to write and express my desires in order to help it manifest so it was extremely amusing when a Paul manifested in my life. About the same time another friend I know, also called Paul, showed up. I realised I needed to be clearer about what I really did want and not what I didn't want.

Getting back to the dark man from March it served my purpose that this manifestation took five months to materialise because in that time I had changed my mind and found out that he has a girlfriend. When thinking about what type of man I wanted I stupidly focused on what I did not want. I did not want someone from my past for starters ... so what did I get? A blast from the past!

MANIFESTATIONS

One night I am sat there in my front room when my friends call me from a pub. They had bumped into someone from my past, someone I had previously been attracted to and vice versa, but I had always been in a relationship and unable to explore so-to-speak. We were both now single. Without thinking about it I told my friend to give him my number and we said our goodbyes. After the call I thought about this man and my intuition / guidance system told me he was not what I was really wanting for myself. However, he phoned me and we chatted. Instead of feeling elated, I felt doubt. He was not the one. The next day he phoned to say he had my friend's purse as she had left it at the pub. My friend had phoned me frantic with worry, but I reassured her that the man from my past had arranged to bring it to my house. When he arrived from the minute he opened the door I knew he was not for me and we had never meant to be together. However, if he had not got my number or I had not been involved would my friend have got her purse back?

Another thing I thought back then. I focused again on what I did not want. I did not want a blonde, blue-eyed man who I would not be attracted to and I confirmed this after the blast/past. Call me shallow, but truthful. I believe that for the perfect relationship all four boxes need to be ticked; Mind, body, spirit and soul. Lo and

MANIFESTATIONS

behold all that shows up for me for the next few weeks are men that are fair. At least I could see the amusing side of this. Focusing on what I do not want only reinforces to the universe that I do want it. You get what you focus on basically.

Another man also appeared after I sent out there that I did not want him. Whilst meditating I was thinking about materialising a clone of *Henry Ian Cusick* (*Desmond* from *Lost*) because he is my ideal man and is absolutely gorgeous. Suddenly an image of this man I did not want, who lives nearby, popped into my mind. Of course my reaction was to push the image away. 'No' I said loudly. I had to chuckle when a few days later this man was on my doorstep asking for a lift. I politely told him no, shut the door and fell about laughing at the joke I had sent myself. All these manifestations so far have shown me that negative things appear quicker than positive. However, I think this is because we habitually think about negative things and our conditioning causes us to run on default. I've also noticed that the things I think about and do not try to manifest actually manifest quickest. So think, let go and then manifestation occurs. Ask for what you want, the universe answers and then you just have to be ready to receive.

MANIFESTATIONS

Already it is evident that visualisation does speed up the creation process, but visualise and then letting go is the key. The universe likes speed. Approximately May 2007 I started to visualise a life with the man of my dreams and since then men are appearing in my life left, right and centre. Another one of my male friends (from my past tut tut past again) says I have put a spell on him. Chuckle. I have faith my *Henry/Desmond* clone is in the process of manifesting in my life and I will continue to believe I am with him already. We are already connected. Throughout this diary you will note that I talk about things as if they have already happened in order to confirm it and show that I have faith.

MY DIARY – SEPTEMBER 2007

MY DIARY

Sunday September 2nd 2007

I had the urge to go to Lepe Beach today. I have been visualising and one of the scenes is at the beach. Also several U-tube videos on the internet that I watch include romantic beach scenes. My vision board has a beach scene. I imagine this is my own private beach. By going to the beach I would learn how to get there and I would also manifest what I had been focusing on (although I did not realise this when I set out to the beach) All the way to the beach I used my intuition/guidance system to help me find the way. The inner voice told me when I had taken a wrong turn. It did take an hour to get there because the map I had printed out off the internet initially led me the wrong way, but on the positive side this route was beautifully scenic. I took pictures of the boats, the sea etc so I can download them onto the pc. At the moment I am enjoying *Bruce Goldwell*'s *Power of Visualisation 5* positive affirmation video. Take a look at U-tube. *Sacred Meditation* is also an extremely good one to resonate with. The music is *Nirvana* by *Eva* and is beautiful.

MY DIARY – SEPTEMBER 2007

Monday September 3rd 2007

The kids went back to school today so I should get more time to meditate and visualise. I have the urge to go over the common, but I have to do other things first. Terrafyah phoned me today to tell me that my car was parked right next to a car with the number plate *Des* on it. She immediately saw the connection to what I am trying to manifest. Not only am I aware, but others also. I have been visualising for approximately two months for the man of my dreams; my soul mate. I have written down a list of qualities I expect and deserve in a man. The men who do not match my desires, allows me to learn exactly what it is that I do want. This helps me to be certain. I did not see the driver of the '*Des*' car, but yesterday I added 'local' to my qualities list. Also I decided my soul mate needed to be coherent. This was decided after a very brief episode with a mumbly man who I could not understand a word from. I have added coherent to my qualities list and physically healthy just to be on the safe side.

Today I have been discussing language and words with my friends. We are trying to rephrase sentences using positive words. Everyday

MY DIARY – SEPTEMBER 2007

speech is negative and we constantly confirm and reaffirm the same negative things. Even our language it seems is set up to imprison our minds. Our habitual ways of thinking and communicating imprison us psychologically. Sod's Law is a phrase which we use all the time and self-sabotage ourselves with. You have to laugh and see the humorous side of this as this is positive.

It has come to my attention that the aristocracy or posh people do not swear or curse the energy or air. Instead of saying 'shit' for example which is negative, they say 'Goodness gracious me'. They send out positive vibes instead of negative. It would be interesting to research this more. Language has changed. When did this begin to happen? Look at William Shakespeare during the Renaissance. Was language not more poetic and colourful back then? Sentences were formed differently in the past. The connotations of words have changed.

Tuesday September 4th 2007

I got a space at Azda today that I pre-ordered. Today was a busy day. I had to go to the job centre, but it was okay because the man who worked there was very friendly and made me feel very good

MY DIARY – SEPTEMBER 2007

about my degree. One of my desires is to be respected. Today I felt respected. My light is shining today because I am sending it out there and I am glowing. I feel young, alive and energised. I am still visualising.

Wednesday September 5th 2007

Today was a beautiful hot day and I spent hours daydreaming about love. I do not think it was a coincidence that I bumped into a lady today who only a few weeks ago told me about a job in a nearby college when she came to my door and noticed my certificates hanging in the hall. Today she told me that unfortunately there was no job vacancy after all because ESOL teachers were no longer in demand due to the fact that the college can not get the funding. Foreign students have to now pay for lessons so there will now be less demand for English language teachers like my-self because not many foreign students can afford to pay. Despite hearing this negative news I did not let it perturb me, although I could not quite fathom out why the coincidences that occurred in the first place had now led me to a dead end. Anyway I went over the common and soaked up the energy and beauty.

MY DIARY – SEPTEMBER 2007

Thursday 6th September 2007

We have been discussing the power of words again. I looked at *Aldous Huxley*'s '*Brave New World*' after it fell off the bookcase at me. In this book I have highlighted about the dead language. Very interesting indeed! I also found another quote about how we are made to be numb, cold, unfeeling which will back up something in my novel that relates to this. My intuition or guidance system is amazing. Meditation does indeed open doors. Today I got a text that was written wrong, but I read it how it was supposed to be written anyhow. How's that for intuition? I have spent time visualising and meditating before bedtime and I must remember to be grateful in the morning. Every day I am finding things to be grateful for. Today my friends and I discussed again how conditioned we are, but if we are capable of learning new languages, then we can certainly learn to reword sentences positively. I need to slow down and choose my thoughts carefully to recondition myself and rewire.

MY DIARY – SEPTEMBER 2007

Friday September 7th 2007

All we see is lack everywhere when living in a financially restricted life.

Reaffirm – Lavish unfailing abundance – I always see lavish abundance.

Today I watched some of *Sai Baba's* work and it was amazing how he manifested things from out of nowhere. Magick!! When reading some of his teachings I found it was much the same as '*The Secret*'. Yesterday I looked up more about magic. I noticed rhyming words are important. Slogans often use three words because this does something psychologically. Orators like *Adolf Hitler* knew the power of words. Rituals in magic exist because if rituals are habitually done, these habitual thoughts, words and actions create manifestation. This allows the brain to build a new network and then it can accept that magic is possible.

Getting back to romance I have had unwanted advances again from the man in March. (Oops as I am writing this I am confirming unwanted advances) He has been trying to get my phone number. Did I put single on my list of expectations/qualities? He has a girlfriend which is a shame. This is definitely why our desires do

MY DIARY – SEPTEMBER 2007

not manifest immediately. In the space of time since the party I have found out this man has a girlfriend so it is a big no no. Oh, before I forget to write this down ... I have been imagining my *Henry/Desmond* pulling up in a Mercedes outside my house and yesterday or the day before a black Mercedes pulled up next to me to ask for directions, but alas it was not my clone of *Henry*. I nearly got it right though. Is this a sign it is on its way? Do I need to be more precise when I visualise? Practise makes perfect. It is exciting to see glimpses of my manifestations happening however random or inconsequential they are. My wishes appear to be manifesting in a myriad of forms. In form, through form and out of form!

I will not give up.

I am grateful God/the universe/the source for my determination and my strength of will.

Today I am trying to be as pure as possible.

22.07pm - I just caught myself in mid-sentence. I was thinking about how we are psychologically imprisoned when using negative language and I was thinking this when I uttered the words 'I can't believe it!' When something is the truth and it shocks us or we do not want to accept it we say 'I can't believe it' even when something positive occurs we say the same 'I can't believe it!' This

MY DIARY – SEPTEMBER 2007

is not a good statement because belief is the key. It is only what you believe. The belief systems we hold in our mind create our reality. These days no one believes anything whether science or religion. How convenient! People only believe the reality they see with their eyes, the negative reality. If people do not believe they create their own reality, then they are not free. This is when I begin to feel compassion for mankind. 'Forgive them father for they know not what they are doing.' Our birthright was stolen from us all. We are all the same underneath, but it is just that some of us are aware. Some of us have woken up. I have come to the conclusion that although it was tragic that throughout my life up until now that I did not know the L O A, past is past and I now know the truth. I can now get rid of the negativity from my life. I can now release all fears because I have nothing to worry about. It is simple. I have simply to focus on what I do want and detach from any negativity and what I do not want. Think only about what you love and hold those loving thoughts. The corruption, discrimination, hate and evil of this world that does exist will simply lose its power and depart from your world if you do not focus on it or perceive your world that way. The negative hold will release its grip. If you only and always love, you are at one with the source/God and you are free. Love conquers all.

MY DIARY – SEPTEMBER 2007

September Saturday 8th 2007

I am grateful for my positive friends Terrafyah (the powerful fire walking Goddess) and Dr Nast-E (the magical music maker) who also apply the L O A. Collectively we are more powerful. Which leads me to think that on a collective scale people could transform the whole world. All those third world countries with lack could begin to focus on abundance, they could visualise their country, the land, in a positive light, knowing it is prosperous, fertile and abundant. If everyone did apply the LOA a new world would emerge, a free world based on love. It is hard to stop focusing on lack when the cupboards are getting empty or the kids are asking for money. It is hard to not confirm to them 'I have no money' when this is the habitual answer. Dr Nast-E thought up a way of dealing with this when his child asks for money. He says 'I have got money, I've just got to find it' Chuckle. I am working on manifesting lots of money using powerswitch video systems that use imagery, audio and visual subliminal switchwords and Alpha-wave brain entrainment techniques to bombard the subconscious and force it to align with the conscious mind to attract things in life you want and desire. Again I will remind my-self that whether I think it is working or not the law of attraction is always working

MY DIARY – SEPTEMBER 2007

and it is therefore inevitable that I am wealthy because I constantly focus on this daily. I know that so therefore it is so. My book is a success. The evidence that the law of attraction is true and does work is already apparent. As I look back at the last three months it is clear that I am attracting into my life the things I focus on whether negative or positive. This is mind blowing. Also it is evident that visualisation plays a very important part and speeds up the process dramatically. The best thing about this is that it is not hard. It is easy and it is great fun.

Also I must write this I was hoping to get certain negative individuals out of my life, but the more I focused on them the more they appeared in my life. I have been focusing instead on love, wealth and happiness in my life now for approximately three months. Yesterday something occurred that prevents these individuals from coming round my house. Something happened that I did not will or instigate something that was inflicted by someone else, but nevertheless benefits me. God does move in mysterious ways. It is not because I dislike or hate these individuals I really do like them. It's just that they do not hold the same beliefs as me and it is time we parted ways. They are not on a spiritual path and I am and therefore these people do not serve my growth any more. I wish them well in their future, but my

MY DIARY – SEPTEMBER 2007

intuition/guidance system warns me not to be involved in their future as it is not in alignment with what I want for myself. Last time I ignored my intuition; my guidance system (which repeatedly warned me) I ended up in a terrible negative situation that I possibly could have avoided if I had listened right back in the first place. Rule for today: ALWAYS listen to your intuition/guidance system!

Sunday 9th September 2007

Last night my mobile phone drowned lol. I have been putting it on the window sill, in order to get a better reception, above the sink. I'm not sure how many times I thought it is going to drop in the sink, but I definitely did at least twice. Lo and behold it fell in the sink and is not working. I also told a fib a few days ago to Paul. Sorry Paul! I said my phone was not working properly so I did not have to talk to him and since saying this my reception has been playing up and now my phone is broken. The fact is that I had confirmed my phone was no longer working several times or that my phone was playing up to people. The law of attraction has yet again been at work. (That will teach me to fib)
Some people might argue or question whether my intuition was guiding me when I had the thought that my phone would fall in the

MY DIARY – SEPTEMBER 2007

sink. Was my intuition warning me it would fall in? Or did the thought create the occurrence? The trouble is by default we choose the worst outcome or scenario instead of the best. When I thought the phone is going to fall in the sink I should have moved it or replaced the negative thought with a positive thought or affirmation? I could have thought of someone I love to counteract the negative, however I forgot and my brain was on default it appears. I was also not grateful for my phone. (Attached to the phone is a memory of my ex as he gave it to me)

At the moment I am getting money in dribs and drabs which I am totally grateful for, but obviously I would like large amounts. Should I start to focus on a set amount of money, for example £100,000 as this is what '*The Secret*' advises. The universe does not know how much money you want unless you tell it and ask so I think I should start to work on a fixed amount of money. However, is this necessary when apparently if you focus always on love everything else will come with it? To be on the safe side I will focus on love and a fixed amount of money to be paid within a certain time period. I love money. I love my hundred thousand pounds.

MY DIARY – SEPTEMBER 2007

One has to take into consideration that this is all new to me. I am a novice experimenting, but again I remind myself that practise makes perfect. I am exploring and learning. Affirmations for today: I have a mobile phone that works perfectly and I have £100,000.

I have been affirming that my son always uses the potty as I am potty training him. My friend and family have also helped to affirm this. Today he has been on the potty twice and yesterday he did too. I have also been confirming that my son speaks coherently and he has improved vastly in the past few months. It is amazing. I must remember to think about and expect the best parts of the children. I must think of all their qualities and send love as this will mean we will live in harmony together. If they are negative then it will not affect me. Affirmation: My children live in harmony together and completely understand and respect one another.

Thursday 13th September 2007

What I am sending out there is certainly coming back. On Tuesday I went round to see a male friend of mine (purely platonic) and he said that loads of men had asked about me. I must say men seem to

MY DIARY – SEPTEMBER 2007

be becoming more attractive. Is this because I am resonating with this vibration and people's inner beauty is revealed? It could be argued that my hormones are playing havoc as it has been five months since I had a boyfriend. Physically my body could be craving. It could be both reasons after all they are both connected. As I focus on attracting love on the inside I become more attractive on the outside. This also means that people will become more attractive to me also. Anyway one of my male friend's friend apparently said I was nice and so I told my male friend to give him my number. However, I'm not sure if this is a good idea considering I saw him briefly and do not know a thing about him. I'm not sure he will pass my number on because he actually wants me all for himself. He has been after me for years, but he is a bit of a player I think and I have always looked at him as a friend only.

I have had a testing few days, but today I have come on so hormones are to blame. Our moods seem to take over. I had to force myself to be positive and do visualisations and affirmations. Terrafyah and I are going to start tai-chi in two weeks which is good as this is all about energy. Getting back to the time of the month for a woman, apparently tribes would send their women into a wigwam on their own during their period. They would be excluded because this was when they were believed to be in their

MY DIARY – SEPTEMBER 2007

power. Whoa! I am powerful!! I am in my power!! I am rich in consciousness, I am rich in manifestation. It is like magic once you know the L O A. The things you do just seem to fall into place. I must get some ink to print my novel. I also have to write a synopsis.

Friday 14th September 2007

I have been grateful this morning. I had a good night last night visualising more romantic love scenes with the man of my dreams. Luckily I am quite obsessive about things. I do not do things by halves. This morning I had to laugh…. I had a look at my emails and a dating site, I joined a month or so ago, had sent me one concerning a new member. Guess what his name was? DESMOND lols. I have printed this out for your information. See Appendix B. There is no such thing as a coincidence in the sense of the word as most people perceive it. What I have sent out there is manifesting in many forms, one of these forms is the correct perfect manifestation; the perfect outcome for the best version of myself. It is only a matter of time now. Again I am grateful that I am aware. It is magical indeed. Terrafyah sent me a very positive

MY DIARY – SEPTEMBER 2007

e-mail that I read too this morning. It was about how to stop negative thoughts. The only way to do this is not to pay any attention to them as what you focus on persists. What you resist persists so let them just drift by. If you constantly focus on positive thoughts, being thankful for everything throughout the day, this is like planting seeds as I have said before. I am just drumming it in to myself as well as you. By doing this, negative thoughts will simply fade away and be habitually replaced with positive ones. One of the affirmations I am now repeating daily is gratitude for my new husband. I say 'Thank you for my husband' whenever the thought or urge arrives. One of the important things to remember, as I have explained before, is that one should always act as if it is already happening. This is having faith. No doubt = Faith. You are ready to receive when you do not doubt.

Going back to what you resist persists; I was finding a lot of acorns and leaves in my garden so I kept throwing them back over the fence. Then this was pointed out to me that because I was throwing them away this was only going to bring more because I was focusing on them by pushing them away. Lo and behold during the next few days acorns and leaves were appearing everywhere tenfold. Thankfully this has now stopped because I have given up and let go. All is good. I stopped focusing on them and blessed my

MY DIARY – SEPTEMBER 2007

garden instead. I constantly look at my beautiful garden and I am very grateful for it. Thank you. Thank you. Thank you.

I am a successful and respected writer. I am a primary school teacher. I have to apply by December 2007 to ensure I get a place on the course as there is so much competition. I have already done a degree and a Cambridge English Language Teaching to Adults course in order to manifest my desires. When my friend and I went to a spiritualist church to get some healing one of the healers there called Derek said that he was getting a message through that spirit wanted me to be a leader and he could see lots of small children around me. He said he knew I had my own children, but this was a larger number of children. Then he said 'they want you to teach'. I have thought for a while now about stepping up the ladder and eventually becoming a headmistress. Obviously I would never give up my writing because this is my true love.

I have a wedding reception to go to on Saturday night. My friend's mum, my soul mum as I call her, told me (a few years back now mind) that I will meet the man of my dreams at a wedding reception. Although she was not sure whether she was actually seeing my wedding or I was with this man at someone else's wedding. She said she could see us standing under chandeliers and

MY DIARY – SEPTEMBER 2007

voiles were blowing in the breeze in the background. My soul mum has made correct predictions in the past. Or is it our belief in them that makes them manifest? This is the question worth thinking about.

Saturday 15th September 2007

Saw my friend who I was supposed to be going with to the reception tonight only she accidentally got the wrong night and we missed it. So we are still going out tonight although I am not sure where we are going. I am driving so I will not be drinking which means we can go somewhere further a field. Go with the flow!! All paths lead to the same place and we are all doing what we should be doing when we should be doing it. I have not heard anything on the romance front. However, I feel very positive today. I have an inner knowing that all is as it should be. I am grateful for my positive attitude. Lavish abundance.

Monday 17th September 207

I have just realised that the positivity seeds I have planted are growing. My two year old was whining and I naturally said 'Cheer

MY DIARY – SEPTEMBER 2007

up! It's a good day today'. The positive thoughts are increasing. Where my son is so young he is like a sponge. It is the perfect time to teach him to be positive by setting a positive example. I would love to be able to control what I say all the time instead of reacting to situations negatively and uttering sentences that are detrimental to our happiness. For example: You children are always arguing. Why do I confirm this time and time again? Now I am aware at least I can do something about this. Back to positivity!

I am waiting for my colleague, from the ESOL teaching course I successfully completed, to send me my teacher's contact details so I can use them as a reference. I can then complete my application for the pgce course I intend to happen. Watched '*What the Bleep do we (K)now!?*' again last night. It is about quantum physics and it certainly helps put everything into perspective. It pulls away the veil. It helps you see through the illusion. Found a school letter this morning from my children's school asking for parent helpers so I have phoned up. I must go in to see the teacher about any hours I could help. Fingers crossed things are happening. Thoughts shape reality! In form, through form and out of form! I had a good conversation with my mum's husband yesterday. He also has been studying quantum physics. Every time we talk about it or are shown evidence that the law of attraction exists, we lift our

MY DIARY – SEPTEMBER 2007

vibrations and build a neuron net in our brains that accepts that anything is possible. It is a lot easier to rewire, obviously, without outside negative influences unless one can stay detached as possible. This is hard when our minds are bombarded with information and the perceptions of others affect us. I enjoy my time alone because it is only my input and I can choose to be only positive. The affirmation for today: I have positive people in my life.

I am destined to have a happy, wealthy and abundant life.

I expect and receive miracles constantly.

I create my life every day with the help of visualisation and positive thoughts.

Wednesday September 19th 2007

My son has a cold. I was worried that he would catch one because he refuses to wear his coat out and the last few days it has been nippy. I confirmed a few times to him that he would get poorly and lo and behold. I hope this was not my fault. We believe that if we get cold we will catch a cold because doctors etc have told us this information. I am not saying it is not true because I am no medical expert, but can we affect others with our thoughts? It sounds

MY DIARY – SEPTEMBER 2007

ludicrous, but other people's perceptions do affect us after all they help create our identity. The person we think we are, although in my opinion this is not our true identity. Take away all those impressions and essentially at the core we find out who we really are. I think if everyone did this then we could discover that at the basic level we are all the same underneath; we are one.

Affirmation: Thank you for my son's healing.

                Thank you for my son's healthy skin.

Today we have been discussing about how we affect other people and we all agree that one can affect how people feel by being negative around them, but our own thoughts create our own reality, not others. In other words if I think evil about another person it would only come back on me. What you think about is what you become. I do not think therefore we can shape other people's realities. It is all you and only you after all. It is wise to stay detached from negative people if possible or they rub off. When the voice is clearer on the inside than those on the outside is when you know you have achieved the goal which is to be a master at creating your own reality.

Today I have got ink for my printer so I can begin to print out my manuscripts. Wahey! Also I have got my reference's email details at last and GTTR have now requested a reference from my previous

MY DIARY – SEPTEMBER 2007

teacher. As soon as they receive the references' replies my application will be forwarded to university. All in all it was a progressive day.

I can honestly say out of all the days I have been putting into practise the law of attraction I have had lots of positive days and only a few negative days here and there. Last week was lavish abundance. We had everything we needed. There was a period before that where lack caused negativity, but this tested my faith. Now if I feel overwhelmed or negative I immediately try to focus my thoughts on positive things. This does work! Music changes your mood. Affirmations also help to change your perspective. If it does not work at first keep persevering. Brainwash yourself. Try meditation. Choose the best possible outcome for yourself by putting yourself in the driver's seat. Quantum physics reveals that all possibilities are available to us, the observer/you decide which one and this is often or not down to a simple thing …. Belief. Our beliefs are attached to memories, unfortunately by default we choose to match up present day experiences with these memories. So if you have always experienced losing for example, by default you will expect to lose. When we become consciously aware of this one can begin to change how one perceives the world around them. Stop running on default and consciously choose your own thoughts.

MY DIARY – SEPTEMBER 2007

Everything around us is apparently an illusion. Everything we see around us is made up of atoms and electrons that rapidly move in and out of our existence. When the creator watching them is not looking they act like waves, when the creator/watcher is looking they act according to what is expected of them. The creator is the watcher creating his or her own reality. We are creators. Getting back to the illusion ... we believe that we live in a mortal body and that one day we will die. That is how intense this illusion is, but the truth is that we have always been alive and have never actually been in a sense alive in the physical, material world we believe is real. We are so convinced it is real that we cannot see that our physical bodies are merely an energy field. Our physical body is made up of atoms, is it not? We can affect our physical bodies with our thoughts and we do this all the time. I advise you to research water and the fascinating discoveries concerning how we affect the water in our body with our thoughts. It will encourage you to love yourself even more. Apparently Madonna only drinks blessed Kabbalah water so it is no wonder she looks so good for her age.

MY DIARY - OCTOBER 2007

Wednesday 3rd October 2007

I have not written for over a week. My son has started playschool so this marks the beginning of a major change. I have been to the dump and got rid of all the baby toys etc marking the end of a stage. This backs up the idea that the outer world reflects the inner world. On the material level (the outer) I have said goodbye to my son's baby toys, on the emotional (inner) level I am letting go of my son's baby stage.

Today I have been discussing the days of the week with my friends and we think that re-naming them is a good idea, especially for people who hate Mondays and all the associations connected with the word so :-

Monday	=	Lavish Abundance Day
Tuesday	=	Even More Lavish Abundance Day
Wednesday	=	Miracle Day
Thursday	=	Awesome Day
Friday	=	Best Day Ever
Saturday	=	Bliss Day
Sunday	=	Gratitude Day

MY DIARY - OCTOBER 2007

We had to laugh because Dr Nast-E has been focusing on not swearing only to find he is swearing more. It has been a lavish abundance week for the past few weeks. I am still getting unwanted advances from men I am not interested in and by writing this I am confirming it once again. Oops!

I have been to a hospital appointment for my pre-op assessment and I have an investigative operation on Monday 8th October. Although we can apparently heal ourselves I believe that doctors and nurses are the energy source/God working through form so one should definitely pursue this form of healing as well as attempting to heal ones self. (stress is the major cause of dis-eases! We could choose to be happy and lead better, stress free lives if we just believe it can happen. Enough faith can heal).

One way I am healing myself is by not allowing men to use me anymore. Now I am single I have promised myself that I will never do this. I think the bad experiences I have had with men have manifested and as a result I have gynaecological problems. If I no longer allow anyone to use me I can respect myself. I allowed myself to be used before because I did not value myself or my worth, but this has changed and as the inner changes so will the outer (my body).

MY DIARY - OCTOBER 2007

Affirmations: I love myself.

        Empowering thoughts empower me.

        Thank you for my new husband.

I am still finding plenty of things to feel grateful for. Today I was grateful for my peace and quiet. Last week was progressive. I have written blurbs, character biographies etc for my novels and fortunately my friend went to the library and stumbled across a book that was perfect for me.

It was advice for writers wanting to get published. This advice probably means the difference between my book getting published or not. I am really grateful for this information and now I am nearly ready to send both submission packages off to an agent in London.
Affirmation: Every day my wealth increases vastly
I have also created two adverts on U-tube which helps to get my novels noticed. You never know!
Affirmation: I am a successful author.

If it is indeed all my reality created by me then I have to marvel at our power. The morning of my hospital appointment I set up every obstacle you can imagine.

MY DIARY - OCTOBER 2007

When I first got up I did not realise it was the 1st October or that I had a hospital appointment but then something triggered my memory.

Then I realised I had no petrol in the car.

Then I realised I had no money for petrol.

I battled between whether I should go or not. I even tried to convince myself I could self heal, however doubt did get the better of me when I reminded myself why doctors and nurses are here. I decided to borrow some money for petrol and go. On the way I am sat at the traffic lights when a lady in a black car screeches to a halt behind me. Strangely I did not feel disturbed in anyway. It was as if I knew she would not hit my car because I was safe. However, the next minute I heard a thud as the woman rolled slowly into my car. She had been doing her make up and hadn't noticed her car rolling forward. This still did not shake me. It was okay, we were safe. At this point I could have chosen to get out of the car and see if there was any damage which I doubted, but I knew this would hold me up for my appointment.

Could this have been another obstacle I had created so I could get out of my appointment? I was sending negativity out there about it after all. Nevertheless I arrived actually early for my appointment which turned out to be lucky. The woman before had not shown up

MY DIARY - OCTOBER 2007

and I went straight in. My appointment was over and done with quickly and I did not even have to wait.

Affirmation: I am the perfection of life.

Thursday 4th October

Wahey! I have sent off letter, blurb, biography of author, characters' biographies, synopsis and the first few chapters of *'Precious'* and *'Please Believe!'* today to the Literary, TV & Film Agency called Blake Friedman. This name was given to me from a friend of a friend. In form, through form and out of form so I feel I must send it to this particular agency as I asked the universe for an agent or publisher and within a few weeks my friend mentioned someone she knew already wrote for this particular agency so she asked him for advice which she got and passed on to me.

Affirmation: I believe in myself.
I am successful and prosperous.

MY DIARY - OCTOBER 2007

Saturday 6th October 2007

My eldest son came running in from football training today excitedly calling me. He said, 'mum mum guess what I have got from the source?'
I guessed that he had scored a goal, but he said no and produced a pair of football boots he had wished for. He did need some desperately and we are both very grateful. Terrafyah and Dr Nast-E have been manifesting a fence very successfully for their garden. My washing machine has finally given up so I have asked the universe for a new one within two weeks as this is a real necessity with all my children. A friend says she can get me one for £60 so on a positive note the affirmation today is Thanks for my new washing machine. I will let you know as soon as I receive it. I am now wishing for the perfect man for me by November 2007 as I felt that maybe I should try to put a time limit on my wish.

Friday 12th October 2007

I have not written this week because it has been a completely mad week.

MY DIARY - OCTOBER 2007

Monday 8th October I had an operation at hospital (knife cone biopsy of the cervix). On the Saturday before the operation I received a phone call from hospital informing me that I was having the operation in the afternoon. This annoyed me because I had already made arrangements to be at the hospital for 7.45am. Everybody was putting their-selves out for me. Mum had to phone her agency and re-arrange the starting date for her new job because she was taking me to the hospital and driving me home after. My friend Terrafyah was coming around at 7.00am so she could babysit the children plus take them to school, look after my youngest son and pick the others up later from school. The letter from the hospital had said 7.45am and I reminded the nurse of this and explained how I could not simply rearrange everything at such late notice. She agreed with me and told me not to worry she would get me on the list for the morning operations.

So Monday morning came and nil by mouth I arrived at the hospital. I asked what time they thought my operation would be and they said they were not sure yet. However, as I sat there I felt completely calm and sure that somehow I was going down to theatre that morning despite outside appearances. The day unit was packed with patients, but contrary to this I remained positive …. I know the secret after all …. So as I sat there I gradually watched

MY DIARY - OCTOBER 2007

people being sent away (refused their ops for various reasons) and two people phoned up and cancelled. Within an hour of arriving I was told I would be going down to theatre second. I could not help but smile to myself that when you know the LOA everything just falls into place. I am very grateful!

After the operation the nurses obviously have to make sure you are fit to go home. I was told by one nurse I could go in a couple of hours, however after two hours had passed this particular nurse had gone to lunch and another was on duty. I asked if I could go and she asked to check how much I was bleeding. When she looked she was not satisfied that I was okay and this panicked me slightly. There was no way I was staying in hospital! At this point I was sending out negativity and a lot of fear. I couldn't stay in I had children to get back to …. I couldn't put on other people any longer…. After about another hour went past the original nurse returned and I said to her I really wanted to go home; I almost begged her. I was angry I had agreed to the operation in the first place. I said if I had known there were any risks from the operation I would not have had it done. Blah blah blah. The nice nurse checked my bleeding again. It wasn't too bad, but she was not entirely happy. However, she agreed to let me go home on the understanding that I immediately returned to hospital if the bleeding

MY DIARY - OCTOBER 2007

got heavier. I was very grateful to be released. I have always compared hospital to a prison as you feel cut off from the outside world and to a certain extent you are not free until your health permits it.

Returning home I felt extremely weak and overcome from the anaesthetics so I lay on the settee until I went to bed. I must have only been asleep a couple of hours when my son woke up and disturbed me. He was extremely irritable due to a cold he had caught. I tried to be patient, but this was hard when I felt so exhausted. My son often wakes in the night still and demands a bottle or he wants to get up and go downstairs so at first I thought he was just trying it on. However, I did as he asked because I did not have the strength to argue and we went downstairs and slept uncomfortably for the rest of the night. I think all in all I had about three hours sleep. The next morning my son's breathing was rapid and he seemed really unwell so despite my body weighing a ton of bricks I decided to get down the doctors with him. He was put on a nebuliser to help him breathe and within minutes he fell asleep. My doctor, the nurse and my-self all agreed that he looked very white. It was extremely worrying. The doctor listened to his chest again and was not satisfied that it was not crackling (a sign of infection or puenomia) so she decided to send us up the hospital. It was all my

MY DIARY - OCTOBER 2007

nightmares coming true and history replaying itself I felt. Obviously I burst out crying as I was frantic with worry. Thankfully my friend Terrafyah drove us to the hospital and reminded me to be positive and apply the law of attraction to my advantage. Your son will be okay, she said. Anyway to cut a long story short by the end of the day my son improved dramatically and he could not wait to go home. The hospital gave him steroids, inhaler etc to go home with. When we got home I took a bath and I said my thank yous to the universe and I tell you what I was so overwhelmingly grateful from the bottom of my heart.

Looking back I remember thinking why have I created all this for myself? Was it a test? It was strange how when we arrived at hospital my son's sats were low, yet by 4.00pm they had returned to 100%. It was as if my son, my-self and Terrafyah had willed him to get better. You can guarantee angels were helping him. I certainly prayed for help. When you are in such a frightening situation and someone you love is involved it is so hard to have faith, but this faith is crucial especially for the person who is ill and needs positive thinking only. Thank you for my son's and my healing. Affirmation: Thank you for my family's good health
        Thank you for mum and Terrafyah

MY DIARY - OCTOBER 2007

The question is did my fear of hospitals and all the stress that comes with it cause these two days to manifest? I would answer yes it probably did. These scenarios have repeatedly come to me. I must stop sending fears out there and I must not focus on it from this day forth. All is well in my world. I create the reality around me with thoughts of pure love and happiness. Good news …. My tutor has completed my reference and my application is now on its way to university, despite the blocks I have come across.

Wenesday 17th October 2008

I shouldn't have focused on spots last night because this morning I woke up with three more. Today has been an amazing day where everything fell into place. It was a friend's birthday so I went out of my way to do him a favour and this really did pay off. Again I watched a sequence of events miraculously occur one after the other and all is good. Have still been getting attention from an admirer, but not the one I want. This is positive because it reminds me that my manifestations will appear in many forms and I will decide the correct one.

I am grateful for my husband!

MY DIARY - OCTOBER 2007

I have been watching more videos online about the Egyptians, UFO's, The Illuminati and crop circles to name but a few. I also came across images of the skeleton remains of giants. Apparently science was proving bible facts. (The Book of Enoch – giants/Nephilim) Perhaps in another book I could write about these subjects and the connections between these. I thoroughly recommend you take a look at *David Flynn's* theories because they are mind blowing eye openers.

Flynn's video '*The Ouroboros Doomsday Clock*' explains the procession of the equinox in detail. He reveals how the Ouroboros (symbolically represented by a snake eating its tail) is in the process of opening. This in effect will allow access to other dimensions; a portal so-to-speak. This process is complete by 2012 when it will be fully open. *Flynn* also reveals one of the most important crop circles ever found in Winchester, England. The ASCII code reveals a message warning the bearers of false promises. The message states there is still time and asks us to BELIEVE there is still good out there!!!

The Mayan Calendar also appeared in the form of a crop circle and this calendar is referred to as a divine, prophetic calendar which ends in the year 2012 (this date is debatable). I have provided links

MY DIARY - OCTOBER 2007

at the end of this diary for you to delve further. *Ian Lungold* explains the TUN calendar and predicts that shifts in consciousness will be taking place every twenty days from February 10th 2011 until October 28th 2012. He also states that we will receive revelations almost every minute during the universal cycle and the acceleration towards universal consciousness. At the moment we are in the galactic cycle of our evolution and evidence of this is appearing every day with UFO sightings and the appearance of crop circles. There are so many different views, opinions and perspectives out there. I remember watching one video that stated that the year 2012 was merely a half way point to the end of the sun's existence. I have even watched videos claiming there is life, plants, trees and artificially created tunnels on Mars. The question is what will you choose to believe? What do you wish to create?

Today I watched some videos on U-tube about Steven Hawkins theories and alchemy. He talked about energy and Albert Einstein's theory E=MC2 Energy = Matter Speed of Light x2
The more energy you put into something the faster and more magnified the results; the manifestation. So magnetise/amplify your thoughts.

MY DIARY - OCTOBER 2007

We were saying today again and wrongly confirming again that negative things appear to come quicker, but this is because we have still got a habituated way of thinking – still on default. Or is this because we believe this? Fortunately the positive are becoming more frequent and I am amazed at the majic.

I got my welcome letter from GTTR today and confirmation that my application has been sent to university. I am successful! I meet my soul mate in 2007.

My washing machine was paid for on Tuesday 16th October so it is on its way. In a sense my wish has come true already. The *Cosmic Ordering Service*, as *Barbel Mohr* calls it, has responded to my wish to have a washing machine within two weeks. Within two weeks it has been bought and paid for and although it is not sitting in my kitchen yet, in theory I own (bought and paid for) a washing machine …. Out there…. On its way …. To my kitchen.

Thank you universe.

Thank you again universe for the beautiful moon tonight. It was dusk and a very yellow half moon hung low in the sky whilst a few misty clouds crossed the front of it. It really did take my breath away. Oh yes and whoever created us is a complete genius. Our brains are hundreds/thousands of times faster than the fastest computers. We really are God-selves. Wake up from the illusion.

MY DIARY - OCTOBER 2007

Take back your power – your birthright!!! The spirit of God within me is the source of my supply and my God-self knows only lavish abundance.

Saturday 20th October 2007

More manifestations are appearing. I received a text message from a kind man at my son's football training. He has offered to pay for my son's training on Thursdays which is really good. At £5 per week that adds up and at this point in time this generous offer really helps. Thank you God!

I watched a google video yesterday about *David Icke – Was he right?* This is very, very interesting and the man is clearly sane. We do live in an Orwellian world where we are controlled, but falsely believe we are free and more and more evidence does suggest that the secret society – The Illuminati (Also referred to as 12 members of the Maji?) – The New World Order – does exist. Although it is a good idea to:-

- expose the truth that the government does indeed know about other ways to provide fuel etc that do not harm the

MY DIARY - OCTOBER 2007

planet, but will not because of the economic factors and their greed.

- To expose their manipulation and the mind control they use over us (media and propaganda)
- To reveal how they have found UFO's and back engineered these. They have actually found out about tapping into the energy field which is the answer to global warming problems.
- To expose the fact that the Vatican has information that it is deliberately withholding about our spirituality. This information would obviously empower us and free us from their control.

But the more we focus on the negative and confirm this is our reality the more energy we give to it and therefore we are trapped in this negative reality we believe exists and does exist because we confirm it every day. It is all we see.

The question was *George Orwell* predicting the future? has been explored many times and it appears he was indeed. However, if we create our own reality could it be that every single person who has ever read his books or his works has helped to create this Orwellian society using our imaginations? Just think on a collective scale the

MY DIARY - OCTOBER 2007

amount of energy that has gone into this idea. Just think how many people envisioned and visualised the Orwellian society with New World Order domination. Questions could then be raised as to the intentions of this book. Was this why the government back then allowed the people to read Orwell's work because they knew this would actually, in fact, help create globalisation? I mean how many people would agree that we live in a democratic society today in Great Britain? The government know that people are not happy with the status quo. More and more laws are passed every day. In fact there are so many that we, the citizens, do not even know what these laws are. How convenient!! Keeping the people ignorant! I would argue how can you break a law if you do not even know it exists? But never-the-less I am sure this would not even be taken into consideration if one did indeed break one of these fascist, dictatorship laws that are giving us less and less freedom and ensuring that the powers that be have more and more control.

Anyway I need to practise what I preach now and continue to focus on the positive. This is hard when my curiosity wants to explore. (Curiosity killed the cat! Another negative saying that psychologically puts off people from being curious or from searching for the truth). Perhaps I should lock myself up in a cave

MY DIARY - OCTOBER 2007

lol and exile myself from this society, this reality, as it is always attempting to distract you from the truth.

2.00pm   It is worth looking at the Egyptians and the hieroglyphics displayed in the pyramids because there are pictures of UFOs, plus our galaxy, that suggest alien life forms have been visiting our planet for thousands of years. One of the planets in the Egyptian drawings we have only just discovered today, so how did they know about this all those years ago? Also various crop circles replicate Egyptian symbols so do you call this a coincidence? Is it a coincidence that the Freemasons and the Illuminati use these symbols? Is it a coincidence that people all over the world have seen UFOs? Anyone with the slightest bit of intelligence can work out that the government have found UFOs (Roswell 1947) and are making replicas.

Have a look at *The Disclosure Project*. In this many brave ex-military men, credible and reputable, confirm this. Getting back to *David Icke*, who believes the Elite secret society that controls the world are reptilian, I would say that there is always a possibility that alien life forms exist out there somewhere. This taboo subject needs to be re-addressed. In my opinion, you are narrow minded and very naïve if you do not realise that somewhere out there in the

MY DIARY - OCTOBER 2007

universe there are other life forms. Do your research thoroughly before deciding what you believe in. Of course you can always choose not to believe as you have freewill and if you are okay with ignorance is bliss that is good too. Obviously it is better not to focus on anything negative so you could always see it in a positive light. For instance some people believe that alien life forms visited earth many thousands of years ago, during the Egyptian's existence, in order to help them save the planet.

David Icke believes that the government/military have found UFOs and these have provided them with the knowledge that we can apparently use the energy field to provide everything we need without harming earth, although this truth is being concealed. Thankfully knowledge of the law of attraction has revealed that we can change this current negative reality we live in and if everyone starts to apply the LOA successfully we can change the world/save our planet and recreate the Garden of Eden; the paradise it was originally intended to be. Remember people will probably say this is nuts to discredit it or me even, but do I care when i can simply focus elsewhere.

When *Nostradamus*, the Mayans etc predicted the end of the world I like to think that they meant the end of this world as we know it.

MY DIARY - OCTOBER 2007

Perhaps they did not mean it is over for good, but it is over for evil. Hopefully it will be the end of our suppression and the beginning of real freedom. All you have to do is unplug and come off default. Watch '*The Matrix*'. It is full of symbolism and metaphors so free your mind.

Everyone surely wants to know the reason we are here. Personally I have a burning desire daily to find out the answers to everything. I think the people of this world have a right to know the truth about everything, but the powers that be will not allow this because they want all the power and want us to be primitive like monkeys. What a laugh that is….. how we are likened to monkeys. How ironic! How much of history is true? We can only make up our own minds about what we choose to believe in and what we do not. It also depends how far down the rabbit hole you wish to go. The truth is out there and every possibility is possible according to quantum physics. Buddhism teaches us that the master always chooses the best possibility every time. Try and remain detached from what you see with the visible eye around you. Have faith and believe in the best possible outcome every time. Visualise the end result. See your-self living in a free new world that is beautiful, harmonious and lavishly abundant. I am still loyal to my affirmations and visualisations daily. All is good and all is well in my world.

MY DIARY - OCTOBER 2007

4.10pm I have lost the back of my ear-ring. It often falls off, but so far I have always found it. Every time it fell off I affirmed that I always find the back of my ear-ring and I would chuckle and think that saying this affirmation works. However, today I have lost it and have not found it. I realised that I was confirming every time verbally 'I have found the back of my ear-ring' or 'I always find the back of my ear-ring' which unfortunately meant that I must have lost it in the first place. Not a good affirmation because I was affirming, unknowingly, that I always lose them in the first place. I focused on it. I must say this is not as easy as you at first think it will be (applying the law of attraction successfully). It is the same as thinking about the planet earth. If you want it to be healed you must try to think of it as if it has never been harmed in the first place. Never focus on the negative or on the global warming as this will only serve to amplify it. Again visualise the desired end result only. Know that the planet is a safe, healthy, harmonic and balanced environment where the only rule is that freedom and love rules.

Also it is not a good idea to watch every thought you have as the amount of negative ones you have at first is disheartening. '*The Cosmic Ordering Service*' by *Barbel Mohr* is a must read that I thoroughly recommend if you want to quickly learn how to put the

MY DIARY - OCTOBER 2007

law of attraction to good use or test whether it works or not. Try and notice, be aware, of any manifestations, magick, coincidences or miracles as this will encourage more and you will create more. All through your childhood you were told stories about magic, fairies, witches, aliens etc and like many children you probably liked to believe it was true. The world was a magical and mystical place full of possibilities. As you grew up you were told this was all a fantasy and that magick was dark, occult, frightening and bad. Look at history and we can see how magic was frowned upon and discouraged. It was a threat to society and the governments claimed it was blasphemous and satanic. People feared magic. Gradually majick was seen only as a fantasy; something unreal. However, I tell you this magick is real and it is far from fantasy. The law of attraction, creating things from thought, can be described as magic.... something else that has been deliberately kept from you. Magic is happening around you all the time whether you think it is or not.

Meditation helps to advance your intuitive skills. It gives you the answers you seek. A friend of mine said that there is a whole library within us where you can go and find whatever information you require. You have only to look within and meditate on it. Yesterday my son made a large crash, bang, wallops in the front

MY DIARY - OCTOBER 2007

room, but before I got up to look in there I already knew what the damage was. It was the glass angel my mum had bought as a gift for me when I had my operation, so I was rather upset when I saw it. Before I saw it I was reluctant to go into the front room because I knew the sight that would greet me. Or was it this thought that caused it to happen? I do confirm time and time again that my son breaks everything.

Affirmation: My son looks after everything.

My son plays peacefully and harmoniously always. He is gentle, calm and patient.

Sunday 21st October 2007

I must have got out of bed the wrong side today and I can not seem to shift the mood I am in which is near to tears. Whether hormones, the moon or whatever is responsible for this, it is very hard when I feel this way to do positive affirmations successfully. It is the feeling provided that the universe responds to. It is no use saying positive affirmations if you do not feel positive and your heart is not in it. It is also hard to not think 'What am I doing wrong?' Or to not question 'what is happening to my order?' If you feel like this, and I will try to take my own advice here, reassure your-self that

MY DIARY - OCTOBER 2007

you have already received your order successfully and try to find the gratitude feeling of having it. Don't worry if you have a bad day (you are bound to at first) because the positive thoughts are more powerful than negative ones and this means that all the positive ones you have had will counteract this negative day or experience.

The hardest thing I find (and I am only focusing on this briefly for the purpose of this diary because I manifest what I focus on) is manifesting money. It does come to me, but in dribs and drabs. This I obviously create and am confirming now. When you have children to clothe and feed, the bills to pay etc, it is extremely hard not to worry about whether the food or money will last the week. I am responsible for my children and I want them to have everything. I am making changes and I intend to improve our lives dramatically for the better. I have the last hurdle to overcome (my final year of teaching?) and I will be successful no matter what I decide to do. I do feel I am worthy of being happy and wealthy after bringing up four children on my own, studying a degree and a Cambridge certificate of English Language Teaching to Adults. To look at my life/world you would not believe that I was so qualified. My dream of a better life started about five years ago when I began university. I must admit I did not know the law of attraction works back then,

MY DIARY - OCTOBER 2007

but in a way I must have used it as I completed my degree successfully. I wonder if I had of known at the time whether I would have achieved a better result. Would I already be successful and rich by now? I can remember feeling I would never achieve what I had set out to do because the odds were stacked against me. Somewhere along the way I gave up on my dream of ever being successful or rich, but now I am back on the path again and I try to think wealthy thoughts as much as possible. Time is the deciding factor so if we want to speed things up then visualise as much as possible. By the time I finish this book, which should be when I have gathered all the evidence of my findings and can conclude, my manifestations will have all appeared. The three I really wish to manifest and I am working on:-

- To successfully publish my books and increase my income substantially
- To get accepted on a post-graduate degree course at university
- To meet my soul mate in 2007/2008

I have to go now as I have to do my visualisations and affirmations. I never give up. I will manifest my desires. I always get what I want.

MY DIARY - OCTOBER 2007

I feel the need to write a list of all the things I am grateful for. This I advise when you feel it is necessary. My intuition/ guidance system was warning me that what I was thinking about was not reflecting what I was wanting for my future.

Affirmation: Negative thoughts disappear every time I think positive ones.

Oops still focusing on the negative. Do you see what I mean?

Reaffirm:

Every time I think positive I create positive experiences.

I habitually create positivity.

I am grateful for my happy, healthy, wealthy life.

I am thankful for my loving, wonderful children.

I am grateful for my amazing, perfect husband.

I am full of gratitude for my car.

I appreciate my home and the warmth and shelter it provides.

I am grateful for my computer, the internet, my laptop.

I am thankful for my positive friends.

I am full of gratitude for my family's good health.

I am thankful for the peace and quiet I experience.

I am grateful for my positive outlook.

I am full of gratitude for the inspirational ideas I receive.

I am grateful for being me.

MY DIARY - OCTOBER 2007

I am very grateful for the wonderful, enjoyable holidays I have every year.

I am truly thankful for my wonderful exciting career.

I am grateful I can work at my own leisure.

I am thankful for all the help I receive.

I am grateful that I am loved and popular.

I am grateful I am successful.

I am full of gratitude for my gorgeous garden.

Whoa I am feeling a lot better now!!!!

I was looking at a site on the internet earlier when I came across a site concerning numerology. From this I found out that my soul number is 22 which is a master number. It said that I would make a great leader and be successful in life. It also said that many people with the soul number 22 were born into poor backgrounds and hardship in order for them to spiritually progress. The next bit I liked. It said '**often these people are given rich husbands/partners to help them succeed and make their presence in the world known.** Often fiercely political and passionate about their spiritual beliefs, if they do not express this to the world and be successful at trying to change it, they can self-destruct'. (The self destruct bit is NOT in my reality!!! All is well in my world).

MY DIARY - OCTOBER 2007

The big question is did I create in my reality this information for myself? Just as I was feeling deflated I rescued myself with the idea of writing gratitude affirmations and sent myself a numerological reading? Anyway the fact remains whether it is our higher self, angels, God, the source or all these that helps guide us, it appears that miracles really do happen no matter how insignificant they may seem. Someone is looking out for us whether it is our-self or not and I have just been sent two little rescue remedies that, in my opinion, prove it.

22nd October 2007

A lavish abundant day! Just felt I should give a bit of advice: Different sources will tell you different ways to put the law of attraction to use to manifest your desires and they will give you different time periods in which to manifest your wish. At the end of the day it is entirely up to you which method you use. Try obviously to choose the one that resonates with you. Your guidance system/intuition will help you decide it.
Choose the one that is most believable to you as belief is very important. Remember there is no right or wrong way. Everyone is right about the methods they use and everyone's perspective is

MY DIARY - OCTOBER 2007

correct. It is all down to you and only you what method you choose or what time limit you want to choose, if any, to manifest your desires by. It is what you believe in!!! Another bit of advice is if you choose to write a diary, like me, to keep an eye on the progress you are making try to only note down the positive manifestations. Do not focus on anything negative. I have done this because I wish to reveal to the reader this information, but I would not recommend it.

Affirmation: Everyday my wealth increases vastly.

        Thank you for my husband.

        I am a successful author.

Wednesday 24th October 2007

Happy Miracle Day!! We were talking about burning off calories yesterday when I remembered that the process of thinking actually burns off calories. Thinking does therefore use energy and again backs up the fact that thoughts are energy and have a frequency.

The magic is working for my friends Terrafyah and Dr Nast-E. Terrafyah manifested a free weekend where she got in touch with her power, trod on hot coals and broke an arrow using her neck.

MY DIARY - OCTOBER 2007

Mind over matter! They also wanted a fence for their garden and have manifested the fence, posts and paint all for free. They have also had a weekend break given to them. I am so happy for them and my-self because I have wonderful positive friends who apply the L O A successfully and totally believe in it. Thank you universe!

I had a really positive night last night. I found a new visual on U-tube with beautiful music by *Merlin's Magic*. It had me tingling all over. This is another thing worth mentioning: our minds get bored very quick and need new information all the time. I have found myself sitting down to do my affirmations using the same visuals every day, but now time has gone on I find it harder to keep my attention on the pictures and words in front of me because my mind keeps wandering off on a tangent. It has grown bored of the current data and now I am allowing new videos, which resonate with me, to manifest. Also since experimenting with the law of attraction a wealth of information is constantly surfacing in my life. Wahey! Lavish abundance!

MY DIARY - OCTOBER 2007

Thursday 25th October 2007

I was watching a television programme and it was discussing crime and the fact that the prisons are overcrowded in this country. I think they said there are about 81,000 prisoners in this country. How does this compare to years ago I wonder? It is not surprising the prisons are overflowing with law breakers when there are so many laws now that they have in effect caused more crime (cause and effect). Another thing you may not be aware of is this – if you have a gas card meter and you pay for your gas as you use it, like myself, watch out if you run out!! All the time you do not have any gas, the gas company charges you. Basically you get charged for having no gas. It is absolutely incredible that this is happening in this day and age. I told a friend this and she said 'They can't do that' and I said 'It looks like they can and they have!' Daylight robbery! Of course in the new world that will emerge, the world most people desire, everyone will be equal and not 95% poor and 5% rich.

We are our own worst enemies. Here I am focusing on negativity again. Do you see how the system gets you? Now I am reprimanding myself for this. We are our own worst critics too. Many of us are too hard on our-selves when in fact we should be

MY DIARY - OCTOBER 2007

gentle, forgiving and understanding of ones self. The key is to love your-self and then everyone else will too. To be human is to err, so bear that in mind before you fill your lives with guilt, fear, regret or anger at your own actions. In the film '*What the Bleep do We (K)now!?*' it reveals how water is affected by thoughts. Water actually contains a memory. A priest blessed some water and under a microscope the water appeared as a beautiful crystal pattern like a snow flake. When some other water in a jar had the word 'hate' stuck on it, this water appeared as a hideous mutated blob. We are 75% water so we actually affect our bodies with our thoughts. Choose your thoughts carefully. Please love yourself and look after yourself. If you habitually hold negative thoughts you are in affect attacking yourself so choose to be positive. Love everything and everyone including YOURSELF! You are so important. Write a list of all your good qualities and what you have to offer the world. Choose a stress free world. More people need to perceive a Utopia. Only the 5% wealthy people in the world do this at the present time and we wonder why our planet is affected. The 95% poor are feeling trapped and live in a dystopia. We need this 95% to realise the trap. Think positive and make positive things happen. The world is as we perceive it. If we create our own reality, on a collective scale we have all helped to create this world with our thoughts. Once this realisation dawns on you refocus.

MY DIARY - OCTOBER 2007

Pass what you know on and watch your life transform into a miraculous abundance of love, prosperity and happiness. Try and find compassion for others. Put your-self in their shoes to see where they are coming from. If you can not do this, then avoid them or situations that are detrimental to your positive vibration until you have mastered creating your own reality. Only focus on people's qualities and then these qualities will shine from them. Remember when you are in a bad/negative mood you tend to come across bad/negative situations or people because you attract it. Be aware of what happens in your day and what you are thinking/feeling about and attracting. If you are attracting negativity in any form it has come from you as you are the creator of your reality. What you dislike about someone else is usually a perception of something you are criticising or judging. When you were a child I expect you learnt about name calling. Someone would call you a name and you would say 'what you say is what you are!' Well there is more truth to this than you know or maybe did not know until it was pointed out to you. Everything is a projection of yourself; a hologram if you like.

Good news. My washing machine is arriving today, tomorrow or the next day. The lady has my number and address. All good

MY DIARY - OCTOBER 2007

things do come to those who wait. People who wait patiently are safe in the knowledge that good always shows up. These people who are not actually waiting, because if you are waiting you are under the illusion that the manifestation is not here already, get what they want. You do not have faith if you sit there impatiently waiting. Wait in the sense that you let go and live only in the moment experiencing joy in all you do.

26th October 2007

During the time that I have been writing this diary I have been adding to my vision board and re-arranging where necessary. I suddenly realised last night that there was no picture of myself on the vision board so I have rectified this and placed myself next to the man of my dreams. I am playing around with the idea that the outer and inner should reflect one another. If the outside world you are part of is contradicting the inner world, your desires, then you need to make steps to correct either the inner or the outer so they match. It is most enjoyable using creativity and as I envision my perfect life I am giving it the energy needed to turn imagination into creation and manifestation. Magick!! Happy Best Day Ever! Affirmation of the day: I always remember my dreams.

MY DIARY - OCTOBER 2007

I would like to remember my dreams. This morning when I woke up I knew I had a good dream, but I can't remember it. Perhaps if I could recall the details of my dreams, they would contain information about my-self. Of course the perfect dream would be the life I envision with my soul mate. A life of love, harmony, wealth and happiness. If I dreamt it would this help it to manifest? My dad is lucky. He always chooses what he wants to dream before he goes to sleep. He controls his dreams. Unfortunately, he does not know how he does it. It just happens. Because it has always happened it is habitual and his brain must have built pathways to a belief system that accepts this is possible. In my opinion, my dad's dreams are again proof that anything is possible. We do have the power. Keep believing. The more miracles you send your-self as proof and the more miracles the universe provides the faster you will rewire and accept that anything is possible. We do create our own reality, Please Believe!! It is simple, but unfortunately we do try to complicate things. We think it's hard and therefore it is. The more we try to stop being negative the more it appears. Chuckle! It is simple – whatever you focus on you attract. I have realised that maybe I have made things complicated for my-self, maybe I am trying too hard. After all this is meant to be fun, not hard work. Try to keep things simple. It is not a good idea to analyse every thought you have or sentence you speak. Let

MY DIARY - OCTOBER 2007

it just happen. Don't make it a task or challenge to manifest your desires. Merely enjoy daydreaming or visualising about what you do want. Again I want to remind you that I have only focused on the don'ts etc because this is an exploration as well as experimentation of the law of attraction. If negative thoughts pop into your head do not give them a second thought. Refocus immediately on someone or something you love until this happens naturally.

Wahey! I have received a phone call from a man about my washing machine today and it's being delivered tomorrow.

Saturday 27th October 2007 1.00pm

I placed my order on the 6th October and asked for a washing machine within two weeks. It was paid for on the 16th October making it ten days after my wish, that I (in theory) owned a new washing machine. Today is the 27th so it has taken 21 days to manifest in my kitchen. Not bad going …. I mean considering everything ….. the cosmos delivers!!

I have been discussing relationships today and how memories of the past can be triggered in some way to resurface bringing with it the

MY DIARY - OCTOBER 2007

feelings and emotions experienced at the time. For instance you are in a relationship and your partner says or does something that triggers an old memory. If this memory is painful the person remembering it can find it very hard to dismiss this feeling/emotion. It affects the way they perceive their current relationship and if they are not careful it is recreated. So how do we escape from the past when memories and random associations lead us back there? I think the first step is having the realisation that the reaction you are having or the emotions you are experiencing belong to the past and are perhaps irrational. Then perhaps choose a positive affirmation or a powerful loving image you can replace the negative thoughts/feelings with every time they surface and they will soon lose their power. As I have said many times the need to refocus is extremely important. Instead of dwelling on your predicament make steps to eliminate any negativity from your mind by choosing to think about positive subjects. Distract the mind. Choose to be happy. Do something that lifts your vibration and puts you in alignment with what you really desire for your-self. Refuse to be ruled by the past.

If you have the determination, the willpower, to be happy then it will be so. I know this works because after my last relationship broke up I simply chose not to think about him and I focused on

MY DIARY - OCTOBER 2007

anything, but him. I threw myself into an internet game. Although I was really upset, hurt etc at first and I went through all the emotions I chose to pull myself together and to get over it. Maybe it was easier for me to get over it because I have been through break ups so many times. Maybe you do get wiser as you get older and learn from mistakes. I now know I can refocus and direct my energies elsewhere when I put my mind to it.

Thank you for my new gorgeous husband who is perfect for me.
Thank you for my vivid dreams that are easy to remember.

Getting back to relationships and the discussion today we agreed that you can not make someone else love you because we all have free will, just as you can not hurt someone else with your thoughts; you can only hurt your-self. On the positive side this means that if you love someone else, you are sending love out there and therefore you should only receive love back. But what if the person you love does not love you back? If this love/positivity is not in the form of the man you love will it manifest in another form possibly or at a later time? We also call this good karma? If this is the case then I must be due an extremely good man. Oops there I go again. I have an extremely good husband!

MY DIARY - OCTOBER 2007

This reminds me, i have not mentioned before that read tarot cards for people and i have been doing this for nine and a half years now. Learning more about the law of attraction momentarily led me to question whether my intuition reveals the future to the enquirer or whether the enquirer believes what the tarot predicts so much that this in turn creates their future manifestations. Almost everyone I have done tarot for has come back to me saying that everything I predicted for them had come true. I have told complete strangers they will get pregnant and it has come true. However, I have also picked up on other individuals that are already pregnant by using the cards. The tarot reveals the past, present and the future so this rules out the possibility that there is no guidance or intuition involved and that the tarot is merely a tool of creation. I reminded myself that I actually find it easier to read people's cards that I am not familiar with because my intuition guides me rather than logic or reason.

I believe that an insight into the future is available to us using the tarot because our present reality simply creates our future reality. Every thought and action today creates our tomorrow. The tarot not only tells the future, it also confirms to people where they are in their life at the present time or any problems or concerns they might have (which I the tarot reader cannot possibly know) so this rules

MY DIARY - OCTOBER 2007

out the idea that the tarot are randomly selected and then from reading them our belief in it as the truth then helps to create the future we are told we will have. The tarot also reveals a person's past so again this also rules out the idea that the tarot is a tool of creation only. Another reason I believe in the tarot as a tool of divination is because it has always told me the truth whether I have liked that truth or not. I have doubted cards I have picked on many occasions, but they have always predicted the truth.

I have recently done a celtic cross spread to enquire about my soul mate, not because I do not believe he is here already, but because I am curious about him and it excites me to see it confirmed. The tarot revealed to me that a man is coming into my life, but I am not sure if it means he is a fire sign (aries, Sagittarius or leo) or it could be referring to the time period –April – Aries – King of Wands. It is harder to read my own tarot. If the reading is not clear, I tend to read into it what I want to. I also saw financial improvements in my life. Thank you. Thank you. Thank you.

I have just received a letter saying my first choice university was unable to offer me a place on the pgce primary school teaching course. My application will now be forwarded to GTTR who will pass it on to my second choice so fingers crossed. I am positive. I

MY DIARY - OCTOBER 2007

am rich. I leave the how to the universe. I have been considering what to do if my second choice is unsuccessful (oops, this means I doubt). If this is the case I have decided to try to do a PG Dip/MSc in sociology as this looks extremely interesting, especially the philosophy part. It would also lead me in the same career direction to teaching at an even higher level. I could even go as far as studying a Phd as this Masters degree would provide me with the entry requirements.

Happy Bliss Day!

I have not received any news yet about my manuscripts. There was a postal strike for about two weeks so you can guarantee the agents have a backlog of post and mss to get through. No news is good news they say.

Sunday 28th October 2007

Today is a special day. Apparently something wonderful is going to happen on this day according to an astrologer who did a reading for me. November 3rd and 7th were also lucky days so we will soon see.

I actually remembered my dream last night (well the end of it anyway) and probably only because it was negative and scary. I

MY DIARY - OCTOBER 2007

dreamt my youngest son and I were going up in a very strange lift. It literally floated up on its own, but it only had three sides of frosted glass to it and there was no door. As the lift elevated to the top of the room my son fell and I watched as he hit his head and lay unconscious. There were no sounds coming from my son and I thought he was dead. Yuk! Horrible!! This must have been a fear dream. We suppress our fears and they have to find an outlet so this fear surfaced in my dream.

Thank you that my son is always safe!!

Let me rephrase what I wished for a few days ago. I always remember my positive dreams only.

19.23pm. I feel a bit flat. The kids have taken over the pc chuckle so I will have to wait to do some affirmations. The children are back to school tomorrow and hopefully my little one will be okay on Wednesday at playschool.

I need to manifest some money because I have got a birthday to pay for and a party and presents ... the list goes on. I have a phone bill deadline to meet.

Thank you universe for the lavish abundance in my life!

Money comes to me frequently and effortlessly.

Thank you for my husband. This time I have found my true soul mate.

MY DIARY - OCTOBER 2007

It is my dad's birthday today so I wonder if that was the special day my astrologer picked up on? I love my dad.

MY DIARY - NOVEMBER 2007

November 3rd Saturday 2007

I have had an extremely busy week. It was my daughter's birthday on Halloween and I did a birthday tea and we went trick or treating. Yesterday my daughter had a birthday party at an adventure play zone. On Halloween I received news back from Blake Friedman rejecting my novels, buy hey this just means I did not believe that they would be my agents or my books were good enough? Perhaps it would have been to unrealistic for my brain to accept that the first agent I sent to would want to represent my work. I have faith my books are published. I am a successful writer/author. Perhaps this was another test of faith? For every season there is a reason. At first the rejection made me doubt my ability to apply the law of attraction successfully. I did not for a moment doubt the law of attraction exists! I am convinced this is true, but I have not quite rewired yet. Habitual thinking will help my brain do this gradually until I believe in my ability to create my own reality easily and effortlessly. Instead of feeling I am not worthy or good enough I must learn to believe in myself and not compare myself to others so that I make myself feel inferior and unconfident.

My God self knows only lavish abundance.

Everywhere I focus I see glimpses of the L O A and evidence that it exists.

MY DIARY - NOVEMBER 2007

I have been bumping into some gorgeous men. Our paths are crossing.

Thanks for my husband. It was inevitable that our paths crossed as we were already connected. I am creating a vision video on U-tube using window movie maker and its great fun. I think I will use the above affirmation on my video. Remember using your creativity is an excellent way to manifest your desires. It is one of the first steps of creation.

Tuesday I am going to send my manuscripts off to several agents. The letter from Blake Friedman did advise me to persevere. If at first you do not succeed try and try again. Where there is a will there's a way. I have now applied to do a PG dip/MSc Sociology course at university so fingers crossed. Go with the flow. If it is my destiny all will fall into place nicely.

November 6th Tuesday 2007

Let's talk about judgement. I have been reading a book called *'Cosmic Ordering'* by *Jonathon Cainer* (HarperCollins, 2006 London) and he says '... that if you ever want more interaction with

MY DIARY - NOVEMBER 2007

your angel, all you have to do is stop judging… and stop fighting!' p87. I started to think about this. It is horrible that we judge each other, but nevertheless we do. When we judge we tend to compare ourselves to the person we are judging. If we run someone down, find fault, it helps us feel better about ourselves. Come on, admit it! For example: if the person is being too bossy we will compare ourselves to that person and kid ourselves that we never boss anyone around so we are a better person. It is amusing to watch people do this when you are aware of the truth which is that what you are actually criticising in another belongs to you. Running someone else down helps people to feel superior to the victim so-to-speak, but what people do not usually realise is that what we perceive in others is merely an extension of ourselves. It is something we dislike about our-self and should really be working on improving or learning from. Judgement in this sense allows us to be aware of our own faults. Judgement allows us to draw comparisons and out of comparisons comes meaning. In my opinion, once we are aware that we are always judging others we can become less judgemental on other people by looking at our own traits and realising that what you are criticising is a part of you.

Constructive lessons can be learnt from our judgemental tendencies. This is a world of duality where meaning is defined through

MY DIARY - NOVEMBER 2007

opposites, through comparisons. This helps us to learn lessons so my advice is to try to judge less harshly and find compassion for others and your-self when you realise it is all you and only you. I think it is impossible not to judge and I think we need to in order to spiritually grow. However, as I said before please do not judge harshly. It is an aspect of your-self. Compassion for others is also compassion for your-self so try to find this if you can not get your head around the fact that the person/thing you are criticising is a reflection of something you perceive to be a flaw about your own character or life.

Another book I would advise you to read is '*A Little Light OnThe Spiritual Laws*' by *Diana Cooper*. My friend bought this for me as a present and I read it some years ago. I picked up the book a few nights ago and we could not believe that everything '*The Secret*' teaches us was already in this book, yet at the time we had read it something did not click inside the way it clicked when we watched '*The Secret*'. '*The Secret*' reveals the law of attraction has been hidden from us throughout history. It uses scientific credible theories to back up the idea that we create our own reality by our thoughts and feelings and in my opinion this is what makes it believable. This is what makes it real!!

MY DIARY - NOVEMBER 2007

10th November 2007

I was asked out by a man Wednesday 7th November. It is someone I already know and he is a friend. I have mentioned him before in this diary. He has text me before and asked me out, but I made out I did not get his text and he never said anything the next time I saw him. However, he has asked me again and I could not say no because I am too soft. I said if I said yes would he let me go to sleep. It was the middle of the night that he phoned me after all. What are some men like? As I mentioned before I have been reading *Jonathon Cainer's 'Cosmic Ordering'* and he states that we do not always get what we wish for in the form we want because our guardian angel/the source/God/our higher self knows what is best for us and often or not we are presented with things that are blessings in disguise. Also guardian angels/God/the source/our higher self or whatever label you give it, does not judge anyone. So the man I have been presented with is, in the eyes of God, perfect?

As far as I am concerned the law of attraction is always working and my desires for a man are attracting opportunities. However, I am now asking my-self the question is my man friend supposed to be the blessing in disguise because I do not think so? He is only

MY DIARY - NOVEMBER 2007

more of what I do not want. Lols how frustrating! Is he some sort of test? I think it is worth remembering at this point that it is okay to say no thank you to cosmic offerings. Keep believing! On '*The Secret*' they advise you to be very specific when visualising what you want. It is good to imagine every detail as vividly as possible. Perhaps I need to take this advice and be more specific when I visualise or perhaps I am too fussy by far, but when one get's to my age you know what you do and do not want. The trouble is we tend to focus on what we do not want and it manifests. I may go out with my male friend, but I doubt it because I do have serious reservations about him. This must be my intuition/guidance system telling me he is not what I am wanting.

According to Buddhism and my tarot doubt, fear, reservations and distrustful thoughts are barriers between you and the source. They must be worn down and eliminated if you are to progress or be at one with the bliss/ the best possible outcome. I used to think this meant ignore doubt, fear etc because it is in the way of your goal, but now I realise it means if you feel these feelings what you are thinking about will cut you off from the source/the best possible outcome so you must choose another path. Because I do not know the answers to my current situation I am going to go with the flow.... I am going to listen to my intuition/guidance system and

MY DIARY - NOVEMBER 2007

not the logical reasoned voice that attempts to rationalise everything through my past and the physical/material reality around the situation/person being presented. I know one thing I am only settling for the best possible outcome. It's all up to me now after all. Empowering thoughts empower me.

I eliminate all negative thoughts daily and only my positive thoughts manifest.

Sunday 18th November 2007

This week quite a few things have happened as evidence that the law of attraction exists. I was thinking about a girl from the past and for some reason she popped into my mind. The next day I happened to see her walking past my car as I waited for my son outside a shop. Thinking back perhaps I should have spoken to her. For someone who is psychic I could have a word with myself sometimes! Anyway the fact remains that I thought about her and then she crossed my path.

On Wednesday night I had a visit from my admirer, but unfortunately his advances were not entirely wanted. My intuition/ my guidance system says no! I did respond to his kiss at first. I

MY DIARY - NOVEMBER 2007

was intrigued to see if he could kiss well and it has been seven months since I have been kissed. Come on give me a break lol! However, there were no sparks and it just did not feel right. I have an ideal man in my mind and my heart that I am already connected to and settling for anything less than my heart's desire would be wrong. It was strange, but I felt almost like I was being unfaithful to my husband who already exists somewhere (in my heart and mind). Thanks for my new wonderful husband. Thank you for offering a possibility through my friend/admirer, but no thank you.

I did not make it clear (to the cosmos) whether I wanted my friend or not because I was not sure, but my intuition was very strong Wednesday night (I was in my power lol) and I am going to heed its warning. I am grateful for my intuiton/ guidance system.
I am not sure what day it was this week, but my two amazing light friends and I have decided to work on manifesting something together. This gives the creation process more power, especially because there are three of us. Three is a very significant number. It creates a triangle. You could research the number three to find out more about the significance of this number, especially where crop circles and UFOs are concerned. Anyway collectively we are more powerful and we have all agreed to try to manifest 50k by 25th December 2007.

MY DIARY - NOVEMBER 2007

I am thinking about creating my own web site so people can sample some of my work, give feed back, add links to educationally fascinating information, book appointments with me for tarot readings etc etc. Speaking of the internet I am still using my vision video plus others and last night I happened to click on my favourite video on U-tube with Desmond from *Lost*, when I suddenly realised my *Angel Lyte*'s magic love vision video was being shown amongst all the Desmond *Lost* videos. Wow, this has really excited me. Whether or not U-tube put my video there because there are two images of Henry Ian Cusick on it (which I doubt because the tags to the video are nothing to do with him) the law of attraction is yet again working in a myriad of forms and everyday I create something that reminds me of this. This is truly magical and practise makes perfect.

I have had a complete makeover this week; new clothes, my nails done and a new hair colour. I am attempting to break out of my mould. Change and transformation! I am what I am. I love my new hair at the moment. In the past I was always worried that if I changed my hair colour from blonde to brunette I would be less attractive, but beauty is within the eye of the beholder. I am attractive and I am sending it out there. It will be interesting to see

MY DIARY - NOVEMBER 2007

if I get treated any different with brunette hair or if I attract more men. Perhaps my new husband prefers brunettes? One thing I am thankful for is no roots.

I got a reply today from my second choice university about a PGCE primary teaching course, but I did not get in. However, all is not lost, apart from my Desmond lol. I have been into university to provide my certificates for the Masters Degree course in sociology instead. My referees have fortunately agreed to help me again. Also I now know that if I do not receive funding for the tuition fees for this Master's degree then my mum has offered to help me pay it. Bless her soul!! Thank you universe! Where there is a will there's a way. Perhaps not getting accepted on the primary teaching courses was a blessing in disguise. Perhaps the Master's degree is serendipity. I am excited about it. I would love to go on to do a Phd after this. Maybe one day I can teach at university about sociology or philosophy. My novel *'Please Believe!'* is based on contemporary society and it raises questions concerning the social life, groups and societies that exist today. It reveals how society influences us and shapes our lives.
I am a successful author.

MY DIARY - NOVEMBER 2007

Fingers crossed that I will hear from university about an interview this week. Actually I will leave the fingers crossed out. This is my reality is it not? I create it. I will hear from university about an interview this week! Onwards and Upwards! Thank you to Dr Adrian Smith for these positive inspiring words.

Oh yes I forgot to write that I have sent off manuscript packages to another two agents this week (8th November 2007). I can't wait. Oops. This means I can wait and I do not want to.

Must only see my books as already published! Must only see the end result!

I have published my books and they are available in all well known book stores. Thanks.

Saturday November 24th 2007

I have not had replies from my books yet and as yet I have not heard from university. Dr Smith was doing a reference for me last Monday, if he got round to it, bless. I should hear soon.

My television has broken so we are using a small one temporarily. Today I am receiving another tv. My daughter's aunty offered it. Bless her! I have also been given lots of clothes for my kids that I

MY DIARY - NOVEMBER 2007

ordered from the cosmos and within days they manifested. The television only took a week.

I had a strange occurrence last night. I woke up groping for my phone because I was dreaming that it was alerting me that I had a text. However, as I came round I realised my phone was silent and I was convinced the dream was a premonition. Suddenly the phone really did alert me that I had received a text.
The most likely explanation is that my phone did alert me about a text several times because I was asleep and did not respond at first. It was the first alert that found its way into my subconscious and triggered a dream that I was receiving a text. Upon waking I was re-enacting my dream which was quite strange. I was not happy when I realised it was the unwanted advances of my male friend again. What you resist persists! I must not push against this as I am now going round in circles. This man will stop pursuing me once I focus my attention totally elsewhere instead of focusing on how I am going to get rid of these awkward unwanted advances. Easier said than done lol! The problem is that I actually considered (thought about) whether I could actually ever find this man attractive. A big no no if you do not want someone. At least I can laugh about my creative errors anyway.

MY DIARY - NOVEMBER 2007

I have noticed that I have had several highly charged emotional negative dreams over the past few weeks and this does lead me to question negativity in relation to *Sigmund Freud*'s theories. *Freud* believed that if we suppress negative thoughts/emotions/feelings then they have to find an outlet whether through dreams, displacement activity, Freudian slips or other avenues. After discussing this I have still not reached any definite conclusions, but I have come up with more questions. If we are always positive and refuse to acknowledge our memories/the past/negativity then will these not surface in some form in our lives as *Freud* suggests or are the negative dreams I have had providing an outlet so they can be released once and for all as my brain becomes rewired and the negativity begins to dissolve? Time is the deciding factor and therefore I will continue to observe my-self and those around me. I can almost sit back safe in the knowledge that magic is always working. The evidence so far should be enough for me to believe this and I do. However, I realise, I am not totally convinced of my ability to be in the driving seat at all times so-to-speak. I know that I have to realise my power, my God-self and maybe I have set myself goals in order to prove this to myself.

Thank you for my own website where I can advertise my work. I have the power.

MY DIARY - NOVEMBER 2007

I am successful.

I am loved.

I am grateful for my husband.

10.45am

I have just received the reference I needed for my master's course in the post so now I am going straight to the post office to post it recorded delivery to the School of Social Sciences.

At least I am aware of the progress of my application which is still in the process. It is good news. I know I should not worry as this self-sabotages me, but I was wondering if the waiting period was not good news I have to admit. ELIMINATE DOUBT!

Refocus: I am studying a Masters degree at university.

MY DIARY – DECEMBER 2007

Saturday 9th December 2007

It has been an interesting two weeks, at least, since I wrote this diary. I am so glad I chose to do this as it really has helped me to be aware of everything going on around me. We now have our television which I am totally grateful for. About a week after I got the television, my computer decided to give up. The electric ran out (I have a key meter) thus the pc went off abruptly without being shut down properly and when the electric went back on my computer would not work. Fortunately, my wonderful friend's boyfriend is good with computers and he realised there was a problem with the power supply. Unfortunately attached to the subject 'power supply' was a negative memory in this kind man's memory bank. He related this to me. He had fixed his girlfriend's mum's computer in the past and needed a power supply, but unfortunately the one they purchased was the wrong size and it was not smooth sailing to say the least.

At this point, when the story was related to me, I should have chose to see the best possible outcome for myself where power supplies are concerned. However, I was not even aware at the time (neither was my friend's b'friend) that this negative piece of information could have an affect on my reality. This is, in a sense, the power of

MY DIARY – DECEMBER 2007

suggestion at work and what you focus on is what you get. It should have come as no surprise to me in the next few days that I happened to purchase a power supply that was the wrong size. I was most unhappy that I could not use my pc to look at my magic love vision video and do my affirmations.

Within those few days a cloud of negativity seemed to sweep over me and applying the secret successfully went out of the window. However, I suddenly realised where I was going wrong and I decided to refocus. This was after the hard drive malfunctioned and I had to find a replacement for that too. Fortunately, I successfully purchased the correct hard drive and it was a great improvement on the last one. Thank you universe! The fact that I went to the same shop I had a happy memory attached to because I had made a successful purchase there before probably helped. What did not help was me and only me blocking the best possible outcome. We are susceptible to impressions until we can master the voice within, until we know thy self inside and out.

Talking of being susceptible to impressions, remember I said I had unwanted advances from an admirer? Yes, well I had spoken about this with my friend and it appears that my daughter had been listening. About a week ago she complained to me that a boy at her

MY DIARY – DECEMBER 2007

school kept trying to kiss her and she did not like it. I did not get too worried as they are only primary school children and it wasn't as if there weren't any dinner ladies on duty at play times that my daughter could complain to. I told her to do this if the boy persisted. However, a week later she was still complaining to me so I had a quiet word in the school office. It was only later that day when discussing this that I realised my daughter had been susceptible to impressions and my manifest unwanted male had now manifested in my daughter's life too. Wow! This is very interesting and I am now seeing evidence of this everywhere.

Dr Nast-E confessed the other day that he was thinking he hoped I would find the perfect man, but unfortunately his negative conditioning thought this would be very hard as it is his belief that most men were beyond saving should I say (no morals etc). At first, i must admit, i thought 'oh great you've stopped me from manifesting my wish with doubt'. However, I quickly chose instead to believe that this was only my friend's boyfriend's belief not mine, God Bless. The evidence that moralistic decent men do exist was stood in front of my very eyes. Dr Nast-E was that proof. The fact that Terrafyah and Dr Nast-E have been together years, are a match made in heaven and proof that harmonic relationships can exist was proof to me that the man of my dreams is real and does

MY DIARY – DECEMBER 2007

exist. Plus I am so powerful! Surely someone else's negative perception could not undo all the positive rewiring in my brain? Maybe if I was not aware of the affect it could have on my reality then it would certainly rub off in my reality. However, like I said before I refuse to believe anything other than what I wish to believe. Living like a hermit is one solution to escaping people's perceptions, but I would advise the other option… know thy self! Do not let other people's perceptions cloud your reality. If they wish to share negative experiences with you try to remain detached and aware it is a negative impression that could affect you if you let it. You could immediately replace any negativity with an image of the best possible outcome for your-self, a feeling of love or a positive thought.

Another word of advice…. Children are powerful as they are innocent and pure. They are extremely susceptible to impressions so be careful what you say around them or make sure they are not eavesdropping. It is vital to teach them to be as positive as possible. They are the future after all and children have vivid imaginations. A part of me wishes I had told no one what I wished to manifest (although I have not told all) because it makes it harder in ways. Although I totally trust my friends, I am lucky, as they would not try to sabotage my dreams intentionally the fact remains that there

MY DIARY – DECEMBER 2007

is a certain amount of pressure to create these manifestations. This is not a good approach. It is supposed to be fun and not hard work. So orders that are created innocently, secretly, out of love, belief and with ease do manifest the quickest? Or is this just my belief again? After all it is only what I believe and it appears that when we focus on fear, are feeling fear, it brings this fear to us so we can confront it head on. The things we fear manifest too. So orders we have placed manifest no matter what, but the form they come in depends on the feeling behind the order/wish.

If you are placing a positive order, but have negative feelings beneath the surface then this order will manifest in a negative form (because it is ordered from a negative emotion). We tend to think 'what is happening to my order? It has not been delivered or manifested', but it has manifested only in a negative form instead. We are constantly making unconscious orders with our thoughts; thoughts are prayers. The conscious and unconscious need to unite!

I had an amazing dream the other night about me and my soul mate. I woke feeling elated. I had asked for this dream and my wish was granted. Now it needs to manifest on the material plane which I know it has already. I am grateful. The future already exists

MY DIARY – DECEMBER 2007

because today is my tomorrow. Therefore I have a wonderful husband.

Thank you. Thank you. Thank you.

I received an email from university confirming they have received all my references and certificates at last and I should hear soon.

I am successful always.

I choose the best version of myself.

Choose your words carefully. I have been working on a pocket guide to using positive phrases, affirmations, sentences and words. Perhaps language should be re-written and dictionaries should only contain positive words. Look out for this book as it is the companion to this diary '*A Magick Reality?*'

Getting back to being susceptible to other people's impressions, if you believe someone else can affect your reality then what will you get? Yes, you will get what you focus on. You are the master of your creations and the key is to be aware at all times of what you are thinking, buying into or believing. It is so simple, yet our rational minds continually try to complicate things. (It is funny how we call this part of our mind rational or logical because it is far from it). Focus only on what resonates with you.

MY DIARY – DECEMBER 2007

I think it is a good idea to discuss religion and different beliefs. Essentially they are all connected and have the same root belief that there is a creator or creative power whether we call it God, Allah, Jehovah, the source. And they all believe love is God, Allah, Jehovah or whatever. Evidence of the law of attraction can be found in the *Bible, Koran, Torah* etc etc. The *Holy Bible* is the book I want to now focus on because I am familiar with this. You only have to read the following quotes to see for your-selves that God gave man free-will, we are all equal and he wanted us all to live a life of abundance in paradise. All we have to do is ask, have faith we will be answered and be grateful.

MY DIARY – HOLY SCRIPTURES

Take a look at the *New World Translation of the Holy Scriptures*

2 Corinthians   9:8 – 9:15   Giving   p1447.

'Thanks be to God for his indescribable free gift.'

Gratitude for God's generosity! God wanted us to live in paradise and be self sufficient. Those who give receive more. What you give out you get back multiplied.

P1222 – p1223 6:25 – 6:34

25 On this account I say to YOU: Stop being anxious about YOUR souls as to what YOU will eat or what YOU will drink, or about YOUR bodies as to what YOU will wear. Does not the soul mean more than food and the body than clothing?

26 Observe intently the birds of heaven, because they do not sow seed or reap or gather into storehouses; still YOUR heavenly Father feeds them. Are YOU not worth more than they are?

27 Who of YOU by being anxious can add one cubit to his life span?

28 Also on the matter of clothing, why are YOU anxious? Take a lesson from the lilies of the field, how they are growing; they do not toil, nor do they spin; but I say to YOU that not even Solomon in all his glory was arrayed as one of these.

MY DIARY – HOLY SCRIPTURES

30 If, now, God thus clothes the vegetation of the field, which is here today and tomorrow is thrown into the oven, will he not much rather clothe YOU, YOU with little faith?

31 So never be anxious and say, 'What are we to eat?' or 'What are we to drink?' or, 'What are we to put on?'

32 For all these are the things the nations are pursuing. For YOUR heavenly Father knows YOU need all these things.

33 Keep on, then, seeking first the kingdom and his righteousness, and all these [other] things will be added to YOU.

34 So never be anxious about the next day, for the next day will have its own anxieties. Sufficient for each day is its own badness.

This part of the scriptures tells us to have faith and not doubt.

Faith = abundance

Doubt = lack

P1223 7:7 – 7:8

'Keep on asking, and it will be given you;

keep on seeking, and you will find;

keep on knocking and it will be opened for you

8 For everyone asking receives, and everyone

seeking finds, and to everyone knocking it will be opened.

MY DIARY – DECEMBER 2007

Tuesday 11th December 20007

If you look back through this diary you will come across my thoughts on UFOs. At around this time I said to my friends that I wished I could see a UFO with my very own eyes and guess what ….. I have experienced a UFO sighting at 1.50am. My son woke asking for his bottle so I reluctantly got up and went downstairs. As I approached the kitchen, which was completely dark, I could not help but notice through my kitchen window that there was a large gold glowing object in the sky. It was beautiful and heavenly and I can remember wondering if Judgement Day had come. I immediately went to the window to try to get a better look. It was a large glowing gold object, way bigger than a star and no way on this earth was it anything like an aircraft. As I looked at it now and then the centre appeared to be a reddy orange. It momentarily stopped glowing as bright and as the glow disappeared I could clearly see the silhouette of a flying saucer. I know it sounds corny and ludicrous, but this was exactly how it looked. It was a very cold frosty night and the sky was clear and starlit. Although I felt this was definitely a UFO I was not totally panic stricken as I thought I would be, but I did have the feeling it could see me. It was aware I knew it was there and I felt this very strongly.

MY DIARY – DECEMBER 2007

As I was only clad in my bra and knickers I quickly went back upstairs as I felt vulnerable. I headed straight back to the bedroom window momentarily debating whether I should wake my eldest daughter, but I decided against this because I was too worried it would disappear. When I looked out I was glad to see it was still there glowing. It would have been impossible for anyone looking up at the sky at that moment to miss this. Looking out in awe I could not take my eyes off it. I still felt it was aware of my interest so I decided to point to it in case it could see me. As I did so the object began to move slowly towards the right and I followed it with my finger until it disappeared from sight.

This experience left me feeling elated. Instead of being scared of it I felt reassured and safe. I felt privileged to have seen such a phenomenon, such a miracle. The next day I shared my story with my friends who thankfully totally believe in UFOs. The fact that a military base is very near raises questions. I need say no more. My wish to see a UFO with my very own eyes was granted. I sent myself that experience. I created the manifestation of a UFO sighting and out of all my manifestations so far this is the most miraculous. I believed and then I saw! This is further evidence, in my opinion, that I am powerful, I am creating my reality, cosmic orders work, the law of attraction is always working. Therefore it is

MY DIARY – DECEMBER 2007

inevitable that everything else I have wished for, thought about, been grateful for or have focused on and affirmed, is manifesting as I write this. Yippee!!!! Thank you universe! Thank you and me! Thank God. God force at God speed!

If you are reading this and you doubt me or think I am lying about my UFO experience or I am mad because you do not believe in UFOs then I ask you this … why on earth would I want to make up something that people would ridicule me for or would call me crazy? If you do not see UFOs or it does not resonate with you because you do not believe then that is fine, but please try to be open enough to see the point I am getting to. What you believe in you create, you can manifest it, in your reality. What you do not believe in simply does not exist. So the person who believes in UFOs is correct and the person who does not believe in them is also correct.

If you are a doubter, but want to be convinced I suggest you look up the fascinating and brilliant philosopher, *David Flynn*, on U-tube. He goes into detail about the particular crop circle, i mentioned before, that was found in Winchester. In fact this is one of the most important crop circles discovered yet! If this doesn't raise your interest ... the message is written in ASCII code and the geometrical

MY DIARY – DECEMBER 2007

measurements involved with blow your mind. The truth is out there and thankfully thousands of us know it.

What a mind blowing day! Absolutely amazing!

Thursday 20th December 2007

Yesterday I received a reply from university concerning my application to do a Master's Degree in Sociology, but unfortunately I did not get in. My Humanities Degree was not an adequate foundation degree for this particular course although I would argue this if I could as I have learnt so much about sociology and many other subjects because Humanities is such a diverse topic to study. Anyhow all is not lost and I remain positive. I could choose to be negative, but I am conscious that this choice/decision is entirely up to me. I am therefore optimistic and positive.

Two days ago I received information from an unexpected source about The Open University. They provide Master Degree courses which can be studied at home and I should be able to get funding towards it as I am a single mother with a low income etc. Oops not a good affirmation! I am a happily married wealthy woman. Anyway I have been online and have looked at various courses with

MY DIARY – DECEMBER 2007

The Open University. This time I have made sure I have the correct qualification required to do a Master's Degree. As I have a Humanities Degree this means I can study a Master's Degree in Philosophy (which ironically was the main subject I was interested in studying in the MA Sociology course that I was turned down) This MA Philosophy would also lead me down the same career path into teaching so I am going to go for it. Unfortunately I can not apply until March, but for every season there is a reason. On the positive side my friends and family would have forgotten about it by then and it will in a sense be a secret because I am not going to remind them.

I am not saying that anyone is trying to sabotage my dreams; I am merely testing to see if keeping things quiet, secret, gives it more power. '*The Secret*' advises you to not tell anyone what you are trying to manifest. I'm almost tempted to tell everyone, except my two dearest friends, that I have given up on trying to apply the LOA successfully, but then again I can not and will not lie if asked. Dilemma!! It's just that without pressure I think it would be easier and it's all about what I think at the end of the day.

I have heard back from ICM Books about my novels, but my work is not in line with what they publish apparently. I am still waiting

MY DIARY – DECEMBER 2007

to hear from Caroline Sheldon who I sent an email to confirm she had received my mss. They assured me they had received it, but it takes several months for them to get through a pile of manuscripts. Anyway I am not worried, I am still positive. Where there's a will, there's a way! A manifestation of £10,000 would be nice. I could pay to get my books published then. Whether you pay before its published or after (to an agent), either way you pay out so to me it is no different. I give and receive graciously!

MY DIARY – JANUARY 2008

1st January 2008

I received a reply from Caroline Sheldon regarding my manuscripts, but they are not interested. On the positive side no one agent/publisher has criticised my work or said it is a load of rubbish. I think now I am going to send three different chapters (the best ones) instead of the first three. I am also considering changing the title of one of my novels to '*Please Believe!*' as this is a contemporary phrase being used and I suspect 'The Real Version' is already a title of a book out there.

Last time I wrote this diary I was considering whether I should just tell people that I had given up on the LOA, but seriously I can not do this. It would be a lie and I do not do lies. I also have a big mouth and can not help but share my life with my friends and family. Fortunately I do not apply for another couple of months to do my course so I can just let go of thinking about it. Every time I have applied to do a course I have found myself almost holding my breath in anticipation of the results. Looking back I did have my doubts about all three courses I have unsuccessfully applied for… I doubted I would get in because of limited spaces on the PGCE courses and I doubted I would get in on the Sociology course because of my qualifications. However, I feel fully confident about

MY DIARY – JANUARY 2008

The Open University course as this information came to me through form and I do have the relevant qualifications.

Today is the start of a new year and this year is the best ever. This is the year I am successful in all areas of my life. This is the year I am wealthy, happy, healthy and wise. This is the year I am with my wonderful husband. Speaking of soul mates since I last wrote I have been in touch with my ex-boyfriend. He saw my daughter and told her to tell me to get in touch with him. So I did and to cut a long story short I spent Christmas Eve with him. It broke my heart when we split up just under a year ago, but he would not commit to me and I wanted more than just seeing a man on a really casual basis, plus he was very unreliable. Anyway since Christmas eve I have wondered is he my soul mate? I know I now need to apply the LOA and be positive. Perhaps I should convince myself that he will change, but then would I want him? We should not expect anyone to change, but then I do not want him to change, I want his unreliability and his perspective on commitment to change. It is important that a man comes to me in freedom. I should not have to spell it out to a man how I expect to be treated as this defeats the whole object. If I applied the L O A I could choose to believe my ex is my soul mate and we are meant to be together, he will settle

MY DIARY – JANUARY 2008

down and spend more time with me… however, I am too scared to get my hopes up as he has made me a million promises before.

Okay so this is my reality and I create it…. Man has free will so I cannot create my ex's reality only mine (but notice how I keep confirming he is my ex). I can choose to not allow him to hurt me again or to walk away. Or I could choose to write a list of his qualities and focus on them, but I can not make his choices for him. Out of my manifestations so far this is one of the best. I did think of my ex sometimes during visualising (whilst luvved up) and I wondered about him. In my eyes he is absolutely gorgeous and I am very passionate about him.

'Whenever I manifest one fantasy I am able to build bigger and better fantasies' Thanks *Bruce Goldwell*. I like the choice of name! However, I need more than just a good looking man. Hang on let me rephrase that. I desire to experience more qualities in a man than just good looks. I have a big list lols.

There I go again talking about manifesting when I should only be talking about my husband in the present tense … as if it has already happened. However, for the purposes of this diary I have to discuss my life, cosmic orders and results. I have to discuss HOW to manifest your soul mate when the reality is I should not even be

MY DIARY – JANUARY 2008

working out HOW. This is the universe's, God's, the source's job. So... back to this again... decide what you want, think about it as if it is already happening and give thanks for it with the total faith that the HOW is taken care of.

Thanks for my husband.

I am grateful for my wealth.

I know one thing for sure because it is inevitable as I focus on it constantly, I am wealthy and I have a wonderful husband whether it is my evolved ex (the best version of him) or not. Everything is as it should be. My life is forever unfolding, leading me to the next experience or discovery. I am going with the flow and quietening the questions in my mind. I must say a big thank you to *Neale Donald Walsh* and his and my *'Conversations with God'*. I recommend you read this book as it is life changing and answers many questions about why we are here.

I have manifested two leather sofas. Wahey! How's that for a manifestation! And a digital camera too! I put my hand on my heart and say to you that this is my truth. The law of attraction exists. Whether you call it cosmic ordering or not what you focus on is what you get. I am so grateful for this magic in my life. This is soooo exciting. Men are manifesting left, right and centre. I have just got to choose.... I was going to say who knows what lays

MY DIARY – JANUARY 2008

in store for me, but then again I know what lies ahead as I get to choose my own reality with the thoughts I choose. It's all good…. Love, love and more love. Give me a couple of years and I will be completely rewired, re-generated. Apparently our cells are totally replaced by new cells every two years so we really are not the same person after this period of time. This is extremely promising.

Saturday 12th January 2008

This has been a productive week! I have had the overwhelming urge to clear up unfinished business so that is what I have done. After careful consideration I have decided to rename my novel. This meant I had to type up the blurb, character biographies and the synopsis again as I do not have a copy on my computer due to my old hard drive giving up. However, all is good now and I am going to send off my mss package again this week. (I have also chosen three of the best chapters as I mentioned before)
I have also sent off my application to The Open University to do a Masters degree in Philosophy. I thought I had to wait until March, but they sent me a letter so I have acted on it. I feel a lot more positive this time.

MY DIARY – JANUARY 2008

On the romantic front I have decided that my ex is not the best reality for me. I nearly got caught up… but he is not for me. I would be accepting less than what I am worthy of and expect. It would feel like I have given up on my dream and I would be taking a giant step backwards. It was good to see him though and to view the situation from an entirely different perspective than a year ago. I feel in control. Wahey! I am only going to accept the best.

I am grateful for my wonderful, loving husband.

I am successful in all areas of my life.

Another thing I want to mention is that as soon as I let my ex back in my life I caught a stinking cold and my positivity plummeted to zero. I felt irritated and stressed basically. This was a big sign that he is not in alignment with what I desire to experience. We are totally on different paths. I mean I would not even begin to try to teach him about the law of attraction or anything spiritual. He is still asleep, God Bless!

To top things off I went to the doctor for anti-biotics, before I caught the cold, for my throat which thinking back was no way as bad as the cold I then caught. Anti-biotics apparently lower your immune system and somewhere this thought tossed about in my mind when I took them as well as the fact that I just happened to be repeating the same pattern as my son who also had an ear infection,

MY DIARY – JANUARY 2008

anti-biotics and then a cold. I clearly remember having the thought that I would go through the same symptoms as my son because I had caught it off him I told myself. The question is if you have a mildly sore throat and you then buy some cough sweets are you confirming you have a bad throat? Is your cough sweet the doubt? Is the cough sweet a way of eliminating doubt… you believe the cough sweet will make your sore throat better, but do you really need it? (The placebos affect?)

Anyway that is enough talk about bad health. I am healthy. Please repeat this affirmation a few times as I do not wish to be held responsible for manifesting illness in your life through the power of suggestion.

21st January 2008

I have sent off my mss today to Jane Conway-Gordon Ltd so fingers crossed. I am waiting to hear about my Masters degree, but I doubt I will hear anything until March. I was hoping for some sort of confirmation however that my certificates and application was successfully received, but I suppose that is doubt again. I realise one thing … I worry too much lol. Today was a positive day. Over the weekend I created another U-tube video. *Angel Lyte*'s magic

MY DIARY – JANUARY 2008

love vision video 2. The affirmations just came to me as did the song which is amazingly inline with them. I love it! Thanks for my wonderful husband. I have faith.

Monday 28th January 2008

I am dying to tell you about a nice surprise I had last week concerning romance. I have been on a dating site a while, but have not so far been interested in anyone who has contacted me. Fussy, I know. However, last Tuesday or Wednesday night I looked on the site and discovered a very handsome man had sent me a message so I replied. To cut a long story short on Thursday night we briefly met just so we could check each other out before we actually took the trouble of planning a date.

Fortunately, I liked what I saw and so did he. Of course now I have to get my hair and nails done ready for our first date which will be this week sometime. We have been chatting on line every day. It's sooo exciting. I thoroughly recommend to my readers that they begin to apply the L O A and manifest their desires. Obviously I do not want to jump the gun with this man because it is very early days, but I know I have to be positive and expect the best. Trust and faith or I could sabotage my dream. I know one thing for

MY DIARY – JANUARY 2008

certain he is absolutely gorgeous. What a manifestation! I really appreciate it! The possibility is there that he is the one. Oops forgot something else significant to tell you. This man is originally from Jamaica and guess where happens to be circled on my vision board. Yes the Carribean. How is that for the law of attraction!

I have just been back on the dating site to have another look at this man and I have had 100 potential matches click on my profile in the last 10 days. How's that for the law of attraction! I'm telling you girls, men seem to be looking at me left, right and centre. You have got to try this. It is like a snowball effect when you keep sending it out there. This could be quite scary lols. Once again I am astounded at the power of the law of attraction. Enlightenment! Another thing this lovely man I have met is in the army. How ironic! I have spent a lot of time over the last six months researching UFO phenomena and its links to the military have been mentioned on more than one occasion, that's putting it mildly. I wonder if this man knows anything about UFOs. I did ask him, but he replied 'Sweet'.

Yesterday I watched *Zeitgeist – The Movie* (a very controversial film concerning religion, 911 and the New World Order) I recommend that you watch this, especially the part about money and the new ID cards (part 3). I agree that people need to wake up.

MY DIARY – JANUARY 2008

All is good anyway once you know the L O A because it can set you free. It could be the answer to everything and the end of our slavery. People must see a new world vision. We are the creators of our reality. Choose love and not fear!

MY DIARY – FEBRUARY 2008

Saturday 2nd February 2008

What a wonderful week of divine interventions, miracles and manifestations. I am truly looked after – total faith. This week and for the last few weeks I had been saying I want to get rid of my car (although I am grateful for it) due to the fact that the MOT expired soon plus the car tax. The car was basically a bit of a banger so I thought to myself the car has to go, but I have faith that I have a new one. Thank you. Thank you. Thank you. During the week I happened to get a knock at the door and I opened it to find the man I exchanged my house with. He had just driven past my car and he noticed the tax was out. This led him to wonder as to whether I was selling it or not. I said I was selling it soon as it happened, but my tax disc was in date and was not due to run out for another month I corrected him. However, he argued that the tax was definitely out of date and I followed him to my car only to find he was correct. The previous out of date tax disc from six months before was facing me. For a minute I thought the man may have been playing a joke so I checked to see if the car was locked which it was. That ruled out that possibility. Perhaps one of the children had moved it around I thought, but when I questioned them and told them how serious it was to play around with the tax disc, they obviously denied it. Fortunately the valid in date tax disc was behind the

MY DIARY – FEBRUARY 2008

offending one and I changed them back over. Of course I immediately realised that if the man had not seen the out of date tax disc he would not have enquired about the car. Also if he had not informed me about the tax I could have got in trouble with the police. What a Godsend this man was! In form, through form and out of form!

A few days later he just happened to drop in again to ask me if I was still interested in selling the car to him. I said yes because I wanted it gone as soon as possible. He asked to look at the engine and I agreed. When he checked the water it was non-existent. I was astonished that I had not blown the car up. I also really needed the car the next day as I had an extremely important appointment to attend. If the man had not come round and checked the car I certainly would not have. This would most likely have led to me breaking down on the way to the meeting I had to attend. Once again I was looked after. In form, through form and out of form! Divine intervention! I can not tell you how much gratitude I felt. Also if the car had seized I would not have been able to sell it. Of course all was good instead. I can see the positivity flowing through my life.

MY DIARY – FEBRUARY 2008

Thankfully my old car is sold now, but before I even sold it I pondered how I would get a new one. I decided not to worry about it and I confirmed that I knew I did not have to worry because God would sort it now we were connected successfully. I had let go of doubt and knew 100 per cent that I could have whatever I desire to experience because I believed, had faith, that the law of attraction works. I must say though I am still not sure whether I am creating all this for myself or God is giving me what I want. The feelings of gratitude are overwhelming and when I feel like this I do feel connected to God. I feel an immense feeling of love. I have felt so happy that I have wanted to cry at the same time. Thank you God, the creator.

Getting back to my new car… I let go and chose to focus on something else. The very next day after the man saved me and my tax disc there was a knock at the door. I opened it surprised to see my daughter's friend's mum. We often chatted up the school and I had mentioned my car was going. She had come round to tell me her husband had two cars for sale if I was interested. They were in good condition, had a low mileage and were bargains. She said I did not have to worry about the money because we could come to some sort of arrangement like paying weekly or something. I was overcome by the generous offer and felt tears well up in my eyes I

MY DIARY – FEBRUARY 2008

must admit. I tried to keep my composure whilst giving her a million thank yous.

So you see dreams can come true and you do not even really have to lift a finger ... just send a wish out there.

With regards to romance watch this space. The army man has had to go away for a couple of weeks (which my tarot informed me before he did). But as soon as he gets back we should meet up I hope.

This is going to be the most amazing year ever. All areas of my life are going to be ... oops ... are wonderful. Good things come to me always easily. My books are published. I am a successful and wealthy author. I appreciate everything.

Another thing that made my daughter and I chuckle was the fact that the man who bought my old car and came to the rescue looks just like the man on my calendar hanging up in my kitchen at the time I sold my car. Once again the law of attraction was at work and solid evidence as far as I am concerned.

Last night I was reading out what *Dr Joe Dispenzer* says to create his day (from '*What the Bleep do We (K)now!?*'). He talks about how he asks for a sign, every day from his-self or the observer, of the things he created to come to him in such a surprising way that

MY DIARY – FEBRUARY 2008

he can not doubt that it comes from the observer whether God or his higher self or whatever. I think I can safely say I am being shown signs every day and it is truly amazing. I just want everyone to be able to do this.

Sunday 3rd February 2008

I have just been typing up this diary onto the computer because the original is handwritten and I have made a fascinating discovery. Okay remember the man in March with the girlfriend? Well when I wrote his name down in this diary I suddenly decided not to mention personal names in the book and I crossed his name out. I put a random name instead. Well guess what ….. the random name I used instead is only (in real life) the name of the gorgeous army man I met. Isn't that crazy!

7th February 2008

I have been typing up this diary and it has come to my attention that when I was applying for the pgce teaching course there were so

MY DIARY – FEBRUARY 2008

many blocks that I should have realised it was not meant to be. I also doubted I would get in on the sociology course because I felt I did not have the entry requirements. It should have come as no surprise when none of these courses manifested. They were obviously not in line with what I really wanted at this time in my life.

I am a successful author.

I am grateful for my new car.

Life is magical and I love it.

8.20 pm Do you remember the postal strike when I sent my mss to a certain agent/publisher who did not publish it? The strike was another block telling me this was not the agent I wanted for me. Wow!

10th February 2008

Fantastic news I now have my two leather sofas thanks to my wonderful mum and step dad. I am very grateful.

I have been online searching for a publisher for this diary and I feel positive. I must pull my finger out and get this typed up this week.

I am a successful writer.

MY DIARY – FEBRUARY 2008

I have spoken to the army man briefly and I am now wondering whether I will hear from him on Valentines Day. It has been a good weekend with a few eye openers. I have made a conscious decision to stop delving into anything to do with corruption or negativity full stop. I feel I have focused on it too much lately and by doing so I am not applying the LOA successfully or to my benefit anyway. I desire to experience an honest, loving, happy life and I must therefore choose to ONLY think about nice, pleasant, positive things. Pro peace not anti-war!

Anyway it is all very well criticising the system, but one has to come up with something to replace it. As you can see I am viewing things from an entirely different perspective today. Things are only as bad as you think they are. There is everything to live for in my world, love is everywhere.

I must stay focused.

Only my positive thoughts manifest because I am the creator of my reality.

I am grateful that I am wealthy.

Thanks for my new car because I love it!

MY DIARY – FEBRUARY 2008

14th February 2008

Today I received a Valentine text from the army soldier. My heart is racing just thinking about him. I am grateful for this man's attention. It is flattering.

I also received about six unwanted texts from my ex. I mean come on you men out there. If you get ignored six times do you not take the hint? Blunt, but the truth. My ex just could not accept rejection I'm afraid.

I have received a reply from Jane Conway-Gordon Ltd, but unfortunately her client list is full and she could not read my manuscript at this time. I liked the reply because she called me an author. Dear Author …. I like the sound of that. Of course I am an author. I am a successful author and my writing is in demand.

I am sending my mss off again and I have nearly completed typing up this diary to date. I intend to be successful one way or another. In five days the soldier man returns ….. I am sooo excited. I have positive sincere people in my life now. Out with the old and in with the new. Change is due. My tarot is very optimistic. I have faith always.

Thanks for my new husband.

Thanks that my children live in harmony together.

All is well in my world. We are extremely wealthy and very lucky.

MY DIARY – FEBRUARY 2008

15th February 2008

I have just been brainstorming my novel and had some amazing inspirational ideas. This fictional science fiction novel will be set in the year 2012 and already I am itching to start it. I am truly grateful for my creative ideas. This will be my fourth book and four happens to be my lucky number. I shall continue to send off all other manuscript packages because I am a successful author.
Every book I write gets better and better.
Everybody is interested in my work.
I am lucky because I work at my own leisure and I get paid vast amounts of money for it.
Love to everyone always.
Here's to a new world, a utopia!
I am grateful for my husband.
I am grateful I am studying a Master's Degree in Philosophy.
I appreciate my new car. I love it!

MY DIARY – FEBRUARY 2008

17th February 2008

Last night the soldier man called me and asked to see me, but he only gave me two hours notice and I had no baby sitter planned. My little girl also had a stomach ache so I was going nowhere. I sent him a text late explaining that I always need notice, but he did not reply. It was very late as I said and he could have gone to bed, but I have a feeling he has doubts concerning me. If I had gone out with him my babysitter would have called me at 10.00pm anyway because this was when my little girl got bad tummy ache. Is this meeting with this man meant to be? There are lots of blocks occurring. Would I truly be happy with the amount of time he could offer me? I already doubt! Doubt = Lack! Should I let go of doubt with this man? If I did this would everything be perfect? I have to refocus. I have a husband who is perfect for me. I must admit I have been looking at other possibilities online. I just want to be treated with respect, taken out for a meal and a drink and have a decent intelligent conversation with someone who is interested in me and not just my body.
I always meet decent, honest men with intelligent minds.

I must have more faith, but my conditioning is causing what I do not want to keep manifesting and I am confirming it again now.

MY DIARY – FEBRUARY 2008

Oops! Perhaps I need to stop worrying about or being suspicious about men's ulterior motives. I am actually quite old fashioned, this I am learning about myself…. So don't beat yourself up when everything appears to not be going to plan because everything is always going according to plan. I have to be available for my husband. I trust in the right outcomes for me. All is as it should be. I trust my higher consciousness. I am protected from users. Oops too much focus on what I do not want again. I am now going to read my list of qualities I expect to find in my soul mate. We are already connected. I am going to stop my mind from wondering now… stop the whys, hows and ifs because these are all doubt. Only my positive thoughts manifest.

I am an expert at manifesting what I want.

I have a wonderful husband.

As you have noticed when you are rewiring there is a bit of negative versus positive going on, but thankfully we know that a positive thought is hundreds of more times powerful than the negative and the goal to become an expert at manifesting what I want, is already achieved.

Again I want to remind you that doubt stops desires from manifesting how you want them, but how much doubt?

MY DIARY – FEBRUARY 2008

If you doubt once is that enough to stop your wish from manifesting? We talked briefly about this last night and we felt that perhaps 3 doubts = 1 positive. So I am sure if you briefly doubt, but let go of the thought and replace it with a positive then all remains good. In '*The Secret*' they more or less say that 1 doubt stops the creation process. If this is so I have to start again where my perfect man is concerned. They also say in '*The Secret*' that if you are positive for 30 days and do not doubt once then your wish will materialise. This time period or any other time period you set I think depends on what you find believable. I believe you can manifest your desires within 30 days because men and possibilities have been manifesting since I started applying the law of attraction carefully. It is important to mention here that before I consciously began doing this I had no romantic advances from anyone. I believed I was never going to find anyone and that I was almost invisible in a sense where men were concerned. So the change in my life has been dramatic. I just need to do a bit of fine tuning now.

I have a wonderful perfect husband who I am happily married to. I am grateful for my new car. I love it!

Just to let you know I am also now writing a pocket guide to using positive words, sentences and affirmations. It also reveals how

MY DIARY – FEBRUARY 2008

negative language actually imprisons our minds and I have given some examples. I felt it would be a good idea to make this pocket book the companion to '*A Magick Reality?*' Perhaps the first 100 people who purchase copies of this diary could get a pocket guide free.

I am a successful author and writer.

My writing and work is in high demand.

Everybody loves reading my books.

I get paid vast amounts of money for writing my fiction and non fiction.

Everywhere I go an entourage of angels and guides surround me.

I have just had a flashback of last night's dream. It seems really insignificant, but I remember seeing a council van pass me in the road and it had my old settee on it. Tomorrow morning, in real life (although this is debatable lol), my old settee is being taken away by the council. Out with the old and in with the new upgrades. Perhaps my dream was confirming this from a place within me because the inner world was certainly mirroring the external world. Both are one! Majic is real and it does exist. Why do you think they burnt all those witches? Magick is fascinating, exciting, amazing and awesome fun.

MY DIARY – FEBRUARY 2008

Oh yes I just want to write again how much I love my friends and show gratitude because I am so grateful and lucky. Their input has been vital in doing this exploration and they really are special light souls.

Tuesday 19th February 2008

I have sent off *'Please Believe!'* manuscript package to The Women's Press who love crime novels. I am going to send off to other agents too this week. I tried to do some photocopies earlier at the post office, but my son was playing me up so I will go back later to finish the job. I have just looked at my Open University course and applications start March 15 2008. I will continue to write this diary until then so you know I have succeeded.

I went online this morning onto the dating site and the army man had been online, but he did not contact me. Oh well my intuition had been guiding me. He obviously was only after one thing when he wanted it. He obviously was not going to put himself out for me, but expected me to drop everything for him at the drop of a hat. At least I found this out before even going out on a date with him. Actions speak louder than words. I need to affirm that I only have

MY DIARY – FEBRUARY 2008

decent, honest men attracted to me who are looking for a companion, best friend, intelligent conversation and love.
I am grateful for my husband who is attentive, honest, loving and kind.

My ex has been in touch, but I told him it is over and it was a mistake letting him back in my life. He has not changed although he insists he is no longer a jack the lad and he wants to settle down now. I have heard it all before and again I repeat actions speak louder than words and I have not seen him since Christmas so what is that all about? He has made no effort what-so-ever so it really is laughable when he tries to convince me that he loves me. Now the trick is to ignore all these negative manifestations which are more of what I do not want and still believe.
I believe I have a gorgeous, perfect for me, husband.
I am so grateful for my car. I love it!

3.52pm Just sent off mss to Jane Judd Literary Agency in London so that is two agents replies I am waiting for. I say waiting, but I am not going to keep waiting for replies to send off the next mss. I will just keep sending copies off to save time as so far I have only tried 5 agencies/publishers and there are hundreds out there. Oooo it's so exciting.

MY DIARY – FEBRUARY 2008

I am a successful, wealthy author.

8.45pm I saw the lady I am getting my car off today and she said it is not ready yet which was what I wished because I needed time for the money to miraculously materialise.

I am grateful for my new car. I love it!

I am optimistic about my husband because it is written in the stars. Ahhh how lovely!

Love and peace to my ex's and I hope that they all find happiness. God bless them.

21st February 2008

Last night I made a u-tube video for '*The Pocket Book of Positivity*'. This means I have seven videos now. I will be spending the up and coming weeks typing up this guide to using positive affirmations, words etc. I want to donate my profits to charity… I already have plenty of money. Tee hee. Lavish Abundance! I love the luxurious 8 bedroom house I live in. The weight of the world on my shoulders is now as light as a feather. I am grateful to the source and my hero.

MY DIARY – FEBRUARY 2008

27th February 2008

I have manifested flu. I suppose now I have given myself something worth complaining about. I am a bit of a moaner I must admit that I complain about everything when I am down and now it looks like I have stressed myself out to the point that I have got flu (Lemsip Max is on the menu) I found things to complain about and now I have more of the same. I am now going to make a conscious effort to stop complaining as I am doing myself no good. I, of course, create my own reality. Yesterday I sent an email to *Namaste Magazine* because they said they advertise work like mine – this diary – so that is good. I also had someone subscribe to my videos. He said he was interested in the power of intention which he is using to become successful. He felt people should help to promote one another. What a nice man!

28th February 2008

2.38pm: I haven't got much time as I've got to get up the school soon, but today I have been busy and last night I had to create an ad for '*A Magick Reality?*' so I could upload it to other sites (I had no copy on my pc) such as MySpace, yahoo etc. I joined TubeMogul

MY DIARY – FEBRUARY 2008

which is a site where you can upload your videos to at least 12 websites in one hit. Looks like I will be busy in the next few days.

I really feel that things are starting to happen for '*A Magick Reality?*' and '*The Pocket Book of Positivity*' and this is inevitable because I intend my books to be published.

I am a successful author/writer.

Thank you that I am now financially wealthy.

I am grateful for my new car.

Thank you for the new buggy for my son (I got given this out of the blue).

I am grateful for all the upgrades.

MY DIARY – MARCH 2008

21st March 2008

I cannot believe I have neglected this diary for three weeks, but I have been busy recovering from flu plus getting my videos all over the internet. Today is Good Friday and indeed it is. I have joined a site called *Squidoo* and I received a good review from a publisher who offered me the chance to publish my work online ... e books. This is really positive. I am not sure of all the ins and outs, but I intend to explore. I have also joined a site based on a book called '*The Intention Experiment*' and I now have other people intending my books to be published and read by thousands of people so that love, joy, light and happiness will surround their lives and be a part of their lives. There are some amazing light souls on this site who are creating their own realities successfully. They have actually mastered it! There are discussions on this site about UFOs, genetical engineering experiments (PLAN ET - GENE SIS), intention experiments etc etc My friend raised an interesting concept. Could these UFOs/Higher Intelligence life forms possibly be us in the future coming back to warn ourselves about the impending doomsday? (Global warming?) It is a good question, but more and more theories convincingly suggest that we are a genetical experiment and that God is not necessarily the form we have perceived for generations. God, the creator, supernatural

MY DIARY – MARCH 2008

beings, alien lifeforms …. It does not matter what label we give it, what matters is love. Were we created out of love? When I experienced a sighting of a UFO I felt reassured by its presence. I actually felt looked after. These beings know everything you are thinking and they communicated through my feelings. Do not ask me how? I am going to explore this subject and write a book on it maybe as I have only lightly touched on this phenomenon in this diary. What I have done is given you some ideas to think about and a list of web sites for you to research. If you are anything like me then you will enjoy exploring this subject for yourself. One can gather information from different sources and then come to your own conclusions.

Over the past few months I have been gathering more information about language for '*The Pocket Book of Positivity*' (which I am going to donate to charity) a good friend pointed out to me that Amen would be a very good way to end an affirmation.
Thank you that I am a successful author, Amen.
Amen means it is so, it is done.
Yesterday I decided to try to get a loan for a car. The lady I was getting the Renault Clio off said the MOT is done now so I need to get cracking on.
I am grateful for my car, Amen.

MY DIARY – MARCH 2008

Thank you for my wonderful, loving husband, Amen.

Talking of romance…. I have had plenty of offers online, but no one recently that I am interested in. Am I confirming I am single by joining a dating site? Well yes I am. Hmmm interesting. Perhaps I should stop looking? Here I go again questioning the HOW. How's it going to happen? Tut-tut. My inquisitive mind tries to do this, but it is naughty lolls. There should be no questions in my mind regarding my new husband, just a deep inner knowing that it is so. I must carry around my list of qualities in my soulmate as this will affect the water in my body. Water is actually affected by thoughts and feelings and positive thoughts are therefore very good for us. Perhaps if I begin to find these qualities within me, then these will reflect in my husband and my world.

On *www.The Intention Experiment.com*, *Judy Lapointe* is intending to distribute water bottles blessed with good intentions to all local schools. These intention experiments do work. It is amazing the power of intention and it is a remarkable discovery that water can be affected this way. Do you realise the full implications of this discovery? Please check out *Dr Emoto's* experiments. The word really does need to be spread. As I have already said before '*What the Bleep do We (K)now!?*' also explores water and the

MY DIARY – MARCH 2008

affects thoughts have on it. Stick love labels on your water vessels/drink containers etc. Try it out!

The Open University registration has begun so I should hear very soon.

I am grateful I am studying a Masters Degree in Philosophy, Amen.

23rd and 24th March 2008

David Wilcox – The 2012 Enigma – www.divinecosmos.com
Please check out this man and his video above. *David Wilcox* explains how the pineal gland can be found at the centre of the brain. The pineal gland can also be described as a third eye. Yes we really do have a third eye! This pineal gland only happens to contain water. Water allows time and space to flip over. In other word this allows us to time travel to different dimensions. The pineal gland is how we connect to the source. When we shut our eyes the light on the outside goes off… this then triggers a light to come on within. This information has been kept from us, but even the Vatican are apparently aware of the importance of this amazing portal we can use to enter different dimensions such as the world of dreams. *Wilcox* claims that replicas of this pineal gland have

MY DIARY – MARCH 2008

already been built on a grand scale to time travel. These replicas or one of them is known as The Looking Glass and this has been used to see into the future. *Wilcox* raises questions about why the government are allowing fluoride to be added to our water supply when this will help to calcify the water contained in the pineal gland and will therefore cut us off from the source permanently.

Ian Lungold - The Mayan Calendar – www.mayanmajix.com - A big wow.

Ian Lungold's videos explain the Mayan Calendars (in particular the TUN calendar – the divine, prophetic calendar) and what this has to do with our consciousness and the year 2012. Watch this as it give the dates of shifts in consciousness and what we can look forward to in the next few years. Magic will be a part of everyday life as we become part of a universal consciousness.

27th March 2008

Good news! I have been accepted on the MA Philosophy course! Wahey, Yippee, Hoorah! Thank you universe I am chuffed to bits. I have had a really good week with lots of laughs. My car is definitely on its way. I have a new car, Amen. I have now applied

MY DIARY – MARCH 2008

for the loan which I intend to receive as soon as. My car was PREsent. I am soooo grateful, Amen.

MY DIARY – APRIL 2008

6th April 2008

Today my two friends and I went to a group gathering to watch '*The Moses Code*' and to meditate at 5.00pm with the intention of helping Jerusalem. We specifically meditated at this time because other groups in the UK plus those in America were also doing this. It was wonderful to meet people with like minds. A lot of what '*The Moses Code*' advised, we had already stumbled across, but it added clarity to this information and gave extra knowledge about how to meditate using certain words. You will have to read or watch '*The Moses Code*' for yourself to find this out. Anyway we chanted the coded words together and meditated for an hour. That hour flew by. (We activated our pineal glands and flipped space and time over, no doubt)

I especially want to thank *Sally Cook* who organized the whole event and successfully manifested our appearance. Thanks to everyone pre-sent who co-created this day. There were some really special people pre-sent at this event. It is my intention that we keep in touch on line. Sally's husband took photos during the meditation and it will be interesting to find out if any orbs were flying about. Dr Nast-E has renamed himself to Dr Namaste now he knows the power of words. I have been using Dr Namaste's binaural tones

MY DIARY – APRIL 2008

meditation cd based on advanced brain wave theories. This cd is being offered for free at **www.*Namastebeatz.com*** and I thoroughly recommend it. It induces vivid imagery and the sound of water trickling feels almost as if it is cleansing your mind. The last two times I meditated I felt a presence.

I am not sure if this is a guide, my-self, the holy spirit or what label to give it, but I am intrigued.

The more I look into language the more convinced I am that *The Bible* was referring to how language has been tampered with rather than how everyone spoke different languages across the globe.

I have watched a few more google videos online worth watching. *Nassim Harimein*'s *'Crossing the Event Horizon'* and *Michael Tsarion*'s *'2012 The Future of Mankind'* had me glued to my seat. I really do encourage you to do your own research and from these different sources one can come to one's own conclusions. You can put all the pieces of the jigsaw together for yourself. Blessings xxxx

This morning was wonderful waking up to the sounds of my ecstatic daughter with a look of sheer delight on her face. Why? It had snowed. Snowed Love!!! Anyone who is familiar with *Dr*

MY DIARY – APRIL 2008

Emoto's experiments will know that when water is blessed with love it looks like snowflakes under a microscope …. Snow equals love therefore. The earth is being blessed and vice versa. We are all the cells of this earth. We are the earth and part of its consciousness. We all agreed it was an appropriate day for it to snow. I am very grateful for the snow, it was most uplifting.

Getting back to '*The Moses Code*', it did touch on something that I had been having trouble with and that is accepting the negative (or what I wrongly perceived as negative) parts of me. Come on let's all admit it. We can all be bitchy, critical, judgemental … the list goes on and on and I find or I should say I found, these parts/aspects of me despicable. I want to be pure, full of love, saintly, however this is easier said than done. '*The Moses Code*' advises one to embrace these characteristics… love them. Love thy enemy! Love everything and everyone. We are every single aspect of everything and everyone. One consciousness! I do totally understand this and when I read *Neale Donald Walsh*'s '*Conversations with God*' he revealed exactly this to me. However, I obviously needed reminding to stop beating myself up and also to stop focusing on this. I am… what a powerful way to start any sentence. We all have to wake up to our God-selves and to the Holy Spirit within. This is the part they did not tell you in Sunday

MY DIARY – APRIL 2008

school. Now do you feel empowered? This was what Jesus was trying to teach us. Why do you think they wanted him out of the way and The Vatican have kept secret hidden information from us?

I agree with *Michael Tsarion* that this is Pluto's influence which is revealing all that is hidden, all truths are being revealed and corruption exposed throughout the world. We are being enlightened in more ways than one. *Tsarion* also reveals how the word Apocalypse actually means 'to reveal'. It is important that people read this and realise that we have a wonderful future ahead of us and not the doom and gloom scenario many predict. If we really do create our own reality and we are co-creating our future, then it is time we joined together united, each and every one of us, intending a new world utopia where we live in perfect harmony with nature and one another. Amen!
Blessings to Tibet!! I have joined the petition like many others and they are in my prayers. Remember that every thought you have is a prayer.

We were saying today how magical it is that the symbols and signs we have stumbled across recently and found out about have actually been staring us in the face for weeks and weeks. For starters in my u-tube videos I use an image of the brain and guess what's staring

MY DIARY – APRIL 2008

me in the face ... yes, the pineal gland... the gateway that allows time travel to other dimensions. This is real folks. Please wake up. Cynicism is out of the door. I mean lols. On my set of key rings what symbol do I have?.... A six pointed star with six love hearts in the middle. These symbols can be used to meditate on and time travel at certain times in the astrological cycle. The internet has a wealth of information with lots of different theories, some extremely convincing with good evidence and witnesses. Some of the top scientists are now working on projects that will allow us to open gateways to other dimensions.

Check out *William Henry* – Stargates and Ascension – on U-tube. This is most interesting indeed. The web is full of fascinating stuff from reputable and respectable sane people. Just remember we all have our individual unique perspective on things and each and every one of our perspectives is correct from its perspective.

Love and blessings to everyone! I want to send a special prayer to my friend **David on MySpace**. It is my intention that you are fully on the mend.

We really should count our blessings everyday.

Thank you. Thank you. Thank you.

MY DIARY – APRIL 2008

My book covers have been designed and I have visualised my books in book form. I am a successful author that spreads love, light and joy through my writing. Amen.

10th April 2008

Yippee!! Today I received good news that I have the go ahead for a loan for my car. I am now waiting for the money to go into my bank for real. I can not tell you what a relief this is when I have four children on tow. My whole life just got a whole lot easier. I am sooo grateful. You should try gratitude… it's an amazing feeling that connects one to the source. Now the big question is 'would I have got a yes decision to this loan IF I had not applied the law of attraction? I will never know unless I press rewind and get to do the whole scenario again from a negative perspective which I am certainly glad I do not have to do. In my opinion applying the law of attraction successfully and choosing to act as if I have already got a car, did in fact work. I did constantly affirm that the red Renault Clio sat up the garage is mine and so it is…. Actually fantastic! I intended to have it and I felt passionate about this. I can honestly put my hand on my heart and say that life has never been better for me. I am soooo lucky. The only manifestation, still

MY DIARY – APRIL 2008

in the process of manifesting, is my wonderful loving gorgeous husband, but I have total faith now … in this moment… that the source really does give you everything. It's just that some things take longer than others to manifest depending on the belief systems you hold. My man arrives in perfect timing… when I am ready. God bless x.

14th April 2008

I have been looking at my Tarot cards – *The Rider Waite* – and I can not believe the amount of symbolism involved in the pictures. The Magician is of particular interest to me because it holds all of the tools for manifesting anything you desire. The Magician is the creator of his/her own reality. The Wand, the Sword, the Pentacle and the Cup are all a part of the process of manifestation. Note the Pentacles are a star surrounded by a circle and pentacles equal manifestation in tarot. The Wands are thought, the Cup represents emotions (energy in motion) and the Swords are action/doing. Here we can definitely see how we can manifest/create matter with thoughts and feelings.

So thought + emotion + action/doing = manifestation

MY DIARY – APRIL 2008

Just like '*The Secret*' tells us. It should be in this order. Not manifestation/external triggers thought and emotion. We have been doing things back to front …. Were doing things back to front, I should say. Of course I expect psychics, tarot readers etc may disagree with the different meanings of the Tarot cards, but the belief belongs to whoever is the interpreter. I taught myself Tarot nearly ten years ago and at the moment I am trying out doing Tarot in my head rather than actually physically using the cards, that I was told were just a crutch. Apparently I do not actually need these cards to read people's future.

Just to remind you that I am still doing positive affirmations and meditation daily. Meditation, when shutting your eyes allows the light on the inside to turn on. The Pineal Gland then kicks into action and the Secretion (SECRET-ION) of various substances (see *David Wilcox* video) takes place. The pineal gland consists of water and through this water we can flip space and time over ….. We can time travel….. Also known as out of body experience … We become connected to the source … We are at one with our creator.
Start becoming aware of the symbols that surround you in your world, home, life. They are always reflecting your inner world. Thank you that I am connected to the love and light always, Amen.

MY DIARY – APRIL 2008

19th April 2008

Yesterday I bought my car. Yippee!! I am sooo grateful. I really am. Today I have been driving it about to get used to it. I can not tell you what a relief it is. It meant I was able to just pop to the doctors for my son without all the aggro of different buses ... it meant I didn't have to drag him onto public transport whilst he felt very ill. Last week I came to the definite conclusion that I really should not be focusing on videos that discuss corruption, the government and the year 2012 in a negative light. Although these are fascinating and I could easily get addicted, I have learnt new information from them, but I need to now refocus on love, positivity and a wonderful future. It does not do to focus on negative subjects even if it is the truth. I started to feel very low, negative and scared over the past few weeks. It sort of crept up on me. I allowed negativity to come into my consciousness and I was becoming distracted. I know I have given you links to watch, but I would advise you only watch them if you feel you are strong enough to handle the truth. Remember to take as much time focusing on positive things if you are going to watch these so it does not rub off in your life. We co-create, I believe, until one has mastered creating his/her own reality which means that no one can affect your reality. You are free from the power of suggestion, which is

MY DIARY – APRIL 2008

always in play whether one realises it or not, once you are in full control.

Thanks that I am always positive, Amen.

I am sooo grateful for my husband, Amen.

It was inevitable that we met as we are already connected, Amen.

Oh yes ... I forgot ... I have found a new publisher and I will be purchasing the ISBN for this book very soon.

I am a successful author. Dreams can come true!!!

23rd April 2008

My book is published. Yes, this book... so before long you will be reading these words.... proof that the law of attraction does exist. I have had wonderful news today. A few days ago I found a publisher that won 2007 best publisher award last year. For some reason this particular publisher resonated with me. I am extremely excited because I get to edit my own book, choose the cover etc, etc. I am cutting out the middle man which means saving a lot of time for my book to reach the book stores. I am not paying to get my book published, but i am paying for the ISBN and marketing packages. However, one must remember to give and receive. This process is very important and I can not stress it enough. Speculate

MY DIARY – APRIL 2008

to accumulate also springs to mind. If you have mastered applying the law of attraction then you know that giving (without worrying about lack) is the key that opens the door to receiving. You are not really open to receive unless you are giving whether giving love, money or whatever form you give in. I am letting go of all doubt. I have let go of all doubt. I have total faith because I am *Angel Lyte* x.

Thank you universe that my book is published, Amen.

Thank you that I am able to apply the law of attraction and resonance successfully; this wonderful gift I have received, Amen. I am also soooo grateful to my mum and step-dad, who are helping to make my dreams come true.

CONCLUSION

As far as I am concerned the law of attraction does exist and we do indeed live in A Magick Reality. I hope that you soon discover this for yourself too. I can honestly put my hand on my heart and say that my whole world has been transformed since successfully applying the law of attraction to my advantage. From a psychological viewpoint some people might say it is positive thinking that has turned my life around and I could not agree more. However, it is not only positive thinking …. it is belief, faith, love and gratitude that allow me to manifest what I wish for.. to create my own reality. One has to remember as well that in order to manifest your desires one has to believe it is possible. Some people find it harder to believe than others and this depends a lot upon how much they have been conditioned. Doubters do not manifest what they want because they do not have faith. Believe in yourself and your amazing abilities because we are all equal and we are all creating this reality together. Write a diary like me and step into the know…. become aware. When you do this you step into a magical realm and you gradually realise that everything around you is a reflection of the thoughts, feelings, emotions (energy in motion) inside of you. Do your research both on the inside and out. I wish you all the luck in manifesting everything you desire. This is our birthright. Love and Blessings.

Angel Lytexxxx

APPENDIX A

Qualities in my soul mate

Successful, mature, grounded, spiritual, intelligent, handsome, wealthy, healthy, sane, attentive, educated, has an excellent sense of humour the same as me, fun, ambitious, content, positive, focused, brave, mentally and physically strong, dark hair and eyes, attractive to me, good-looking, looks like Desmond/Henry Ian Cusick, confident, supportive, understanding, kind, gentle, passionate, coherent, creative, loyal, generous, interesting, loving, my match sexually, I am irresistible to him, special, musical, talented, patient, calm, we have a deep bond, we know, open, communicative, on the same level as me, knowledgeable, important, determined, masculine, gentlemanly, well-mannered, popular, happy, intuitive, faithful, devoted to me, loves animals and my children, affectionate, has good morals, enthusiastic, energetic, powerful, can apply the secret, honest, helpful, 30 to 45 years old, marriage material, suave, sophisticated, charming, doting, dedicated, responsible, has an accent I love and understand, has an excellent memory, forgiving, deep, experienced, stable, secure, trustworthy, lovable, available, single, sexy, approachable, the perfect match for me, my soul mate, I am his soul mate, friendly, we are best friends, admirable, jammy, fortunate, lucky, magic, adaptable, has good taste in food, clothes and cars, sociable, inspiring, unconditional love, we love the

APPENDIX A

same music, caring, comforting, safe, grateful, wonderful, rich in consciousness, rich in manifestation,, my dream lover, enduring, resilient, courageous, optimistic, imaginative, tactful, dependable, wise, reassuring, truthful, genuine, sincere, desirable, miraculous, heavenly, God-like, caring, merciful, magnificent, logical, rational, exciting, open-minded, loves holidays with me, romantic, sensual, sympathetic, he knows how to love me without being told, he is my equal, unprejudiced, he is my other half, we are connected, we are one, he makes great decisions, masterful, reasonable, he can meditate, he is always there for me, he is full of romantic surprises, complimentary, encouraging, he treats me like a princess, he is my king, I am his first priority, he is my knight in shining armour, he is self-disciplined, he loves me for who I really am, he is firm, but fair, he is financially successful, he is a leader, he is his own boss, he works at his own leisure, he has all the time in the world for me, consistent, enlightening, local, tolerant, gardener, protective, within a reasonable distance, has a driving license.

APPENDIX B

Hey,

Have you seen DESMOND? He's new and I think he could be just what you have been looking for!

Click on the link below to checkout DESMOND's profile.

Good Luck!

Lots of love,

Katherine x x

We at DreamsDiscovered take your privacy very seriously and realise sometimes you may wish not to receive emails for whatever reason. Therefore you can switch the New Player Email notification off at any time. You can always switch them back on again when you are ready by visiting the site and choosing 'My Profile', scroll to the 'opt ins' section link and switching 'New Player Email' to yes. If you do not want to receive any more of these notification emails at present, use the link below (or copy/paste the whole of the link into a browser). Please do not reply to this email. This mailbox is not monitored and you will not receive a response. For assistance, go to the DreamsDiscovered site and click the "HELP" link situated on any page. If you wish to delete yourself, in which case you will no longer be matched on the site or sent emails.

LINKS, INTERESTING SITES AND BOOKS WORTH READING

http://uk.youtube.com/AngelLytexxxx

www.piczo.com/AngelicaLyte

www.namastebeatz.com

www.namastepublishing.co.uk

David Flynn - The Ouroboros Doomsday Clock Part 1 to 9 U-tube

David Flynn - 2012 judgement day and the mars/earth connection on U-tube

Zeitgeist - The Movie on google

The Disclosure Project – on google

http://www.whatthebleep.com/create/

What the Bleep Do we (K)now!? - Written, directed and produced by Mark Vincente

The Secret – Rhonda Byrne

David Wilcox – The 2012 Enigma (google video) –

www.divinecosmos.com

Michael Tsarion – 2012 The Future of Mankind – google video

Ian Xel Lungold – The Mayan Calendar (search google) –

www.mayanmajix.com

Vera Stanley Alder – The Fifth Dimension

Neale Donald Walsh – Conversations With God

Diana Cooper – A Little Light On The Spiritual laws

Lynne McTaggart - www.TheIntentionExperiment.com

Barbel Mohr – The Cosmic Ordering Service

LINKS, INTERESTING SITES AND BOOKS WORTH READING

David Icke – Was he right? – google video

Dr Emoto's Experiments – Search the web

James Twyman - The Moses Code

More Books By Angelica Lyte

The Pocket Book of Positivity – the companion to A Magick Reality?

Precious – a fast paced fictional thriller

Please Believe! – the sequel to Precious

Angel Lyte's work is available at http://stores.lulu.com/angelicalyte

Lulu, Amazon, Barnes & Noble, Borders and British Libraries.

www.ingramcontent.com/pod-product-compliance
Lightning Source LLC
Chambersburg PA
CBHW022012160426
43197CB00007B/395